W9-CFY-423

Chocolate

Chocolate

Over 100 temptingly-tasty dishes

This edition published in 2010
LOVE FOOD is an imprint of Parragon Books Ltd

Parragon
Queen Street House
4 Queen Street
Bath BA1 1HE, UK

Copyright © Parragon Books Ltd 2007

LOVE FOOD and the accompanying heart device is a registered trademark of
Parragon Books Ltd in Australia, the UK, USA, India, and the EU

All rights reserved. No part of this publication may be reproduced,
stored in a retrieval system, or transmitted, in any form or by any
means, electronic, mechanical, photocopying, recording, or otherwise,
without the prior permission of the copyright holder.

ISBN: 978-1-4075-6669-6

Printed in Indonesia

Designed by Fiona Roberts
Photography by Mike Cooper
Home Economy by Sumi Glass and Lincoln Jefferson
Introduction text by Linda Doeser

NOTES FOR THE READER
This book uses imperial, metric, and U.S. cup measurements. Follow the same units of measurement
throughout; do not mix imperial and metric. All spoon measurements are level; teaspoons are assumed
to be 5 ml and tablespoons are assumed to be 15 ml. Unless otherwise stated, milk is assumed to be
whole, individual vegetables such as potatoes are medium, and pepper is freshly ground black pepper.
Recipes using raw or very lightly cooked eggs should be avoided by infants, the elderly, pregnant
women, convalescents, and anyone with a chronic condition. Pregnant and breastfeeding women are
also advised to avoid eating peanuts and peanut products. The times given are an approximate
guide only. Preparation times differ according to the techniques used by different
people and the cooking times may also vary from those given.

Contents

Introduction

"Blissful," "heavenly," "divine," or even "to die for"—words of praise we immediately associate with this magical foodstuff. However, chocoholics of the twenty-first century are far from the first people to regard this unique, indulgent treat as precious and associate it with paradise. In the eighteenth century, the Swedish botanist Carolus Linnaeus, who devised a scientific system for classifying plants, named the cacao bush from which chocolate is produced *Theobroma*—food of the gods. But cocoa beans were also highly valued by the native people of Central and South America centuries before any European landed on its shores.

The Mayan people not only ate the sun-dried beans, probably ground to a paste and possibly mixed with water, but cultivated the bushes on which they grew. Depictions of the god *Ek-chuah* processing cocoa still exist today and it is also known that the Mayan people used the beans as a form of currency for trade before their civilization severely declined around 900 AD. Farther north in what is now Mexico, the Toltec people also valued the sun-dried beans and when they were conquered by the Aztecs in 1325, cocoa beans became the currency of the new empire.

The World's Favorite Confectionery

The chocolate of today is very different from that of pre-Columbian America. The Aztecs had discovered that if the beans fermented before they dried in the sun, they had a less bitter flavor, and they also developed techniques for crushing, roasting, grinding, and mixing the fat-rich cocoa paste with cold water. Chocolate was now a drink, served to kings and princes in gold cups.

In the sixteenth century, the Spanish conquistadors began to flavor the drink with spices from Spain and regarded it as a stimulant that improved the endurance of soldiers. It then became fashionable in Spain itself and its Caribbean colonies, but nowhere else, until the Italians became aware of it 100 years later and began to import cocoa beans. From there the fame of this now hot rather than cold drink, sometimes made with milk, spread throughout Europe. Fashionable chocolate houses appeared in all the major cities from Vienna to London and poems were written in praise of this elixir.

The transformation from drink to confectionery could not begin until the dawn of the Machine Age. Separating out the cocoa butter was the first stage in 1828, patented by Dutchman C. J. van Houten, and other developments followed, but it was Swiss confectioners who produced the first real "eating" chocolate.

Types of Chocolate

The quality of chocolate depends on the quality of the raw ingredients and on the manufacturing process. As a general rule, the higher the percentage of cocoa butter, the better the flavor and texture of the product—and the higher the price. Good chocolate should be even in texture with no grains or specks and should have a distinctive chocolate taste rather than a flavor of cocoa. It should melt on the tongue and not feel sticky or greasy. With the exception of couverture (see below), all types of chocolate are made in varying quality.

* Milk chocolate has added milk solids, usually about 14 percent, and milk fats. It is quite sweet with up to 55 percent sugar. It is light brown in color.

* Semisweet chocolate is dark brown and only lightly sweetened.

* Bittersweet chocolate is very dark, sometimes almost black, and is very lightly sweetened.

* Couverture is always high-quality semisweet or bittersweet chocolate designed for cooking, frosting, and making confectionery. It has a high percentage of cocoa butter, which makes it very workable, but it must be tempered before use. This involves heating and cooling to specified temperatures and then working the chocolate with a metal spatula.

* White chocolate is not strictly chocolate because it is made from cocoa butter but contains no cocoa solids. It is more accurately known as white confectionery coating, but you are unlikely to see it advertised in this way on supermarket shelves.

* Chocolate glacé has a high proportion of vegetable fat and is low in cocoa butter. It melts easily and is low in price, but the flavor is poor and it is not recommended for the recipes in this book.

* Cocoa powder is usually unsweetened and is widely used in baking. Drinking chocolate is not a substitute because it has a much milder flavor and contains sugar.

Chocolate Heaven

Chocolate Fudge Cake

SERVES 8

To make the frosting, put the chocolate, sugar, butter, evaporated milk, and vanilla extract in a heavy-bottom pan. Heat gently, stirring constantly, until melted. Pour into a bowl and let cool. Cover with plastic wrap and let chill for 1 hour, or until spreadable. Preheat the oven to 350°F/180°C. Grease and line two 8-inch/20-cm cake pans with parchment paper.

To make the cake, put the butter and sugar in a bowl and beat until light and fluffy. Gradually beat in the eggs. Stir in the corn syrup and ground almonds. Sift the flour, salt, and unsweetened cocoa into a bowl, then fold it into the cake batter. Add a little water if necessary to make a dropping consistency. Spoon the cake batter into the prepared pans and bake in the preheated oven for 30–35 minutes, until springy to the touch and a skewer inserted into the center comes out clean.

Let the pans stand for 5 minutes, then turn out the cakes onto wire racks to cool. When the cakes are completely cooled, sandwich them together with half of the frosting. Spread the remaining frosting over the top and sides of the cake, swirling it to give a frosted appearance.

¾ cup unsalted butter, softened,
   plus extra for greasing
scant 1 cup superfine sugar
3 eggs, beaten
3 tbsp corn syrup
3 tbsp ground almonds
1½ cups self-rising flour
pinch of salt
⅓ cup unsweetened cocoa

FROSTING
8 oz/225 g semisweet chocolate,
   broken into pieces
½ cup dark brown sugar
1 cup unsalted butter, diced
5 tbsp evaporated milk
½ tsp vanilla extract

Chocolate Ganache Cake

SERVES 10

Preheat the oven to 350°F/180°C. Lightly grease and line an 8-inch/20-cm springform cake pan with parchment paper. Beat the butter and sugar together in a bowl until light and fluffy. Gradually add the eggs, beating well after each addition. Sift the flour and unsweetened cocoa together, then fold into the cake batter. Fold in the melted chocolate.

Pour into the prepared pan and smooth the top. Bake in the preheated oven for 40 minutes, or until springy to the touch. Let the cake cool for 5 minutes in the pan, then turn out onto a wire rack and let cool completely. Cut the cooled cake into 2 layers.

To make the ganache, place the cream in a saucepan and bring to a boil, stirring. Add the chocolate and stir until melted. Pour into a bowl, cool, then chill for 2 hours or until set and firm. Whisk the mixture until light and fluffy and set aside.

Reserve one-third of the ganache. Use the rest to sandwich the cake together and spread over the cake.

Melt the cake covering and spread it over a large sheet of parchment paper. Let cool until just set. Cut into strips a little wider than the height of the cake. Place the strips around the edge of the cake, overlapping them slightly.

Pipe the reserved ganache in teardrops or shells to cover the top of the cake. Let chill for 1 hour.

¾ cup unsalted butter, plus
  extra for greasing
¾ cup superfine sugar
4 eggs, lightly beaten
1¾ cups self-rising flour
1 tbsp unsweetened cocoa
1¾ oz/50 g semisweet
  chocolate, melted
7 oz/200 g Chocolate glacé,
  to decorate

GANACHE
2 cups heavy cream
13 oz/375 g semisweet chocolate,
  broken into pieces

Chocolate Truffle Torte

SERVES 10

Preheat the oven to 425°F/220°C. Grease and line a 9-inch/23-cm springform cake pan with parchment paper. Put the sugar and eggs in a heatproof bowl set over a saucepan of gently simmering water. Whisk together until pale and resembling the texture of mousse. Sift in the flour and unsweetened cocoa and fold gently into the batter. Pour into the prepared pan and bake in the oven for 7–10 minutes, or until risen and firm to the touch.

Take the cake out of the pan and place on a wire rack to cool. Wash and dry the pan and replace the cooled cake in the pan. Mix together the coffee and cognac and brush over the cake. To make the truffle filling, put the cream in a bowl and whisk until just holding very soft peaks. Put the chocolate in a heatproof bowl set over a saucepan of gently simmering water until melted. Let cool. Carefully fold the cooled melted chocolate into the cream. Pour the chocolate mixture over the sponge. Chill until set.

To decorate the torte, sift unsweetened cocoa over the top and remove carefully from the pan. Using strips of card or wax paper, sift bands of confectioners' sugar over the torte to create a striped pattern. Cut into slices with a hot knife to serve.

SPONGE
unsalted butter, for greasing
1/4 cup superfine sugar
2 eggs
1/4 cup all-purpose flour
1/4 cup unsweetened cocoa
4 tbsp cold, strong black coffee
2 tbsp cognac

TRUFFLE FILLING
2 1/2 cups whipping cream
15 oz/425 g semisweet chocolate,
broken into pieces

TO DECORATE
unsweetened cocoa
confectioners' sugar

Chocolate Cake with Syrup

SERVES 12

Preheat the oven to 375°F/190°C. Grease and line a deep 8-inch/20-cm round cake pan with parchment paper. Place the chocolate, butter, and coffee in a heatproof bowl and set over a saucepan of gently simmering water until melted. Stir to blend, then remove from the heat and let cool slightly.

Place the whole eggs, egg yolks, and sugar in a separate bowl and whisk together until thick and pale. Sift the flour and cinnamon over the egg mixture. Add the almonds and the chocolate mixture and fold in carefully. Spoon the cake batter into the prepared pan. Bake in the preheated oven for 35 minutes, or until the tip of a knife inserted into the center comes out clean. Let cool slightly before turning out onto a serving plate.

Meanwhile, make the syrup. Place the coffee, sugar, and cinnamon stick in a heavy-bottom pan and heat gently, stirring, until the sugar has dissolved. Increase the heat and boil for 5 minutes, or until reduced and thickened slightly. Keep warm. Pierce the surface of the cake with a toothpick, then drizzle over half the coffee syrup. Decorate with chocolate-covered coffee beans and serve, cut into wedges, with the remaining coffee syrup.

1/2 cup unsalted butter, plus
   extra for greasing
8 oz/225 g semisweet chocolate,
   broken into pieces
1 tbsp strong black coffee
4 large eggs, plus 2 egg yolks
1/2 cup superfine sugar
generous 1/3 cup all-purpose flour
2 tsp ground cinnamon
scant 1/2 cup ground almonds
chocolate-covered coffee beans,
   to decorate

SYRUP
1 1/4 cups strong black coffee
1/2 cup superfine sugar
1 cinnamon stick

Marble Cake

SERVES 10

Preheat the oven to 350°F/180°C. Grease a 6-cup/1.7-liter ring mold. Put the chocolate and coffee in a heatproof bowl set over a saucepan of gently simmering water. Heat until melted. Let cool. Sift the flour and baking powder into a bowl. Add the butter, sugar, eggs, ground almonds, and milk. Beat well until smooth.

Transfer half of the batter to another bowl and stir in the vanilla extract. Stir the cooled soft chocolate into the other half of the batter. Place spoonfuls of the 2 batters alternately into the ring mold, then drag a skewer through to create a marbled effect. Smooth the top. Bake in the preheated oven for 50–60 minutes, until risen and a skewer inserted into the center comes out clean. Leave in the mold for 5 minutes, then turn out onto a wire rack to cool.

To make the frosting, put the chocolate, butter, and water in a heatproof bowl set over a saucepan of simmering water. Heat until melted. Stir and pour over the cake, working quickly to coat the top and sides. Let set before serving.

1 cup unsalted butter, softened,
   plus extra for greasing
2 oz/55 g semisweet chocolate
1 tbsp strong black coffee
2 cups self-rising flour
1 tsp baking powder
1 cup superfine sugar
4 eggs, beaten
1/2 cup ground almonds
2 tbsp milk
1 tsp vanilla extract

FROSTING
4 1/2 oz/125 g semisweet
   chocolate
2 tbsp unsalted butter
2 tbsp water

Rippled Chocolate Gâteau

SERVES 10

Preheat the oven to 375°F/190°C. Oil and line two 7-inch/18-cm shallow cake pans with parchment paper. Cream together the butter, sugar, and vanilla extract until light and fluffy. Stir in the eggs one at a time, adding a little flour after each addition. When all the eggs have been added, stir in the remaining flour and the ground almonds. Add 1–2 tablespoons of cooled boiled water and mix lightly to form a smooth dropping consistency.

Melt the 1 oz/25 g of chocolate in a heatproof bowl set over a saucepan of gently simmering water. Stir until smooth, then pour over the cake batter and gently mix in a figure-eight action. Take care not to over-mix or the rippled effect will be lost. Divide between the 2 cake pans and smooth the tops. Tap them lightly on the work counter to remove any air bubbles.

Bake in the preheated oven for 25–30 minutes or until golden and the tops spring back when touched lightly with a finger. Remove from the oven and leave for 10 minutes before transferring to a wire rack and discarding the parchment paper. Let stand until cold before frosting.

To make the frosting, break the chocolate into small pieces and place in a heavy-bottom saucepan. Add the butter and maple syrup. Heat gently, stirring frequently, until the chocolate has melted and the mixture is smooth. Add the sugar and stir gently until the mixture is well blended. Let stand until cool and beginning to thicken. Beat occasionally during this time.

Split each cake in half and use one-third of the cooled frosting to sandwich the 4 layers together. Spread an additional third around the sides of the cake and roll in the toasted slivered almonds. Spoon the remaining frosting on top and spread with a swirling action to give a decorative effect. Sprinkle with the chocolate shavings and serve.

1 tsp sunflower oil, for oiling
¾ cup unsalted butter or
  margarine, softened
1½ cups superfine sugar
1 tsp vanilla extract
3 eggs, beaten
1 cup self-rising flour
¼ cup ground almonds
1–2 tbsp cooled boiled water
1 oz/25 g semisweet chocolate

FROSTING

8 oz/225 g semisweet chocolate,
  broken into pieces
5 tbsp unsalted butter
2 tbsp maple syrup or corn
  syrup
½ cup dark brown sugar

TO DECORATE

¼ cup slivered almonds, toasted
chocolate shavings

Mocha Layer Cake

SERVES 8

Preheat the oven to 350°F/180°C. Lightly grease three 7-inch/18-cm layer cake pans.

Sift the flour, baking powder, and unsweetened cocoa into a large mixing bowl. Stir in the sugar. Make a well in the center and stir in the eggs, corn syrup, oil, and milk. Beat with a wooden spoon, gradually mixing in the dry ingredients to make a smooth batter. Divide the cake batter among the prepared pans.

Bake in the preheated oven for 35–45 minutes, or until springy to the touch. Let cool in the pans for 5 minutes, then turn out onto a wire rack to cool completely.

For the filling, dissolve the instant coffee in the boiling water and place in a bowl with the cream and confectioners' sugar. Whip until the cream is just holding its shape. Use half of the cream to sandwich the 3 cakes together. Spread the remaining cream over the top and sides of the cake. Lightly press the grated chocolate into the cream around the edge of the cake.

Transfer to a serving plate. Lay the caraque over the top of the cake. Cut a few thin strips of parchment paper and place on top of the caraque. Dust lightly with confectioners' sugar, then carefully remove the paper. Serve.

unsalted butter, for greasing
1¾ cups self-rising flour
¼ tsp baking powder
4 tbsp unsweetened cocoa
½ cup superfine sugar
2 eggs
2 tbsp corn syrup
⅔ cup sunflower oil
⅔ cup milk

FILLING

1 tsp instant coffee powder
1 tbsp boiling water
1¼ cups heavy cream
2 tbsp confectioners' sugar

TO DECORATE

1¾ oz/50 g chocolate, grated
marbled chocolate caraque
confectioners' sugar, for dusting

Chocolate Madeira Cake

SERVES 8-10

Preheat the oven to 350°F/180°C. Lightly oil and line an 18-cm/7-inch cake pan with nonstick parchment paper. Sift the flour and baking powder together and set aside.

Cream the butter with the sugar until light and fluffy, then gradually beat in the eggs, adding a little of the flour after each addition. When all the eggs have been added, stir in the remaining flour together with the ground almonds. Sift the drinking chocolate powder into the mixture and stir lightly.

Spoon the batter into the prepared cake pan and smooth the top. Bake in the preheated oven for 50-55 minutes, or until a skewer inserted into the center of the cake comes out clean. Remove from the oven and let cool before removing from the pan and discarding the parchment paper. Leave until cooled.

For the frosting, sift the confectioners' sugar and unsweetened cocoa together into a mixing bowl and make a hollow in the center. Place the butter in the center. Mix with sufficient hot water to form a smooth spreadable frosting. Coat the top and sides of the cake with frosting, swirling it to give a decorative effect. Dust with confectioners' sugar.

1 tsp sunflower oil, for oiling
scant 1/2 cup self-rising flour
1 tsp baking powder
1/2 cup unsalted butter or
 margarine, softened
1/2 cup superfine sugar
3 eggs, beaten
1/4 cup ground almonds
1 cup drinking chocolate powder
1 tbsp confectioners' sugar,
 to decorate

FROSTING

2 cups confectioners' sugar
1 1/2 tbsp unsweetened cocoa
2 tbsp unsalted butter
3-4 tbsp hot water

Almond & Hazelnut Gâteau

SERVES 8

Preheat the oven to 375°F/190°C. Grease two 7-inch/18-cm layer cake pans and line with parchment paper.

Whisk the eggs and superfine sugar in a large mixing bowl with an electric mixer for about 10 minutes, or until the mixture is very light and foamy and a trail is left when the whisk is dragged across the surface.

Fold in the ground nuts, then sift the flour and fold in with a metal spoon or spatula. Pour into the prepared pans.

Scatter the slivered almonds over the top of one of the cakes. Bake both of the cakes in the preheated oven for 15–20 minutes, or until springy to the touch.

Let cool slightly in the pans. Carefully remove the cakes from the pans and transfer to a wire rack to cool completely.

Meanwhile, make the filling. Melt the chocolate in a heatproof bowl set over a saucepan of gently simmering water. Remove from the heat, and stir in the butter. Let the mixture cool slightly. Whip the cream until just holding its shape, then fold in the melted chocolate until mixed.

Place the cake without the extra almonds on a serving plate and spread the filling over it. Let the filling set slightly, then place the almond-topped cake on top and chill for about 1 hour. Dust with confectioners' sugar and serve.

unsalted butter, for greasing
4 eggs
$\frac{1}{2}$ cup superfine sugar
$\frac{1}{2}$ cup ground almonds
$\frac{1}{2}$ cup ground hazelnuts
$\frac{1}{3}$ cup all-purpose flour
$\frac{1}{2}$ cup slivered almonds

FILLING
$3\frac{1}{2}$ oz/100 g semisweet chocolate
1 tbsp unsalted butter
$1\frac{1}{4}$ cups heavy cream
confectioners' sugar, for dusting

Mississippi Mud Pie

SERVES 8

To make the pie dough, sift the flour and cocoa into a mixing bowl. Rub in the butter with your fingertips until the mixture resembles fine bread crumbs. Stir in the sugar and enough cold water to mix to a soft dough. Wrap the dough in plastic wrap and let chill in the refrigerator for 15 minutes.

Preheat the oven to 375°F/190°C. Roll out the dough on a lightly floured counter and use to line a 9-inch/23-cm loose-bottom tart pan or ceramic pie dish. Line with parchment paper and fill with dried beans or baking beans. Bake in the oven for 15 minutes. Remove from the oven and take out the paper and beans. Bake the pie shell for an additional 10 minutes.

To make the filling, beat the butter and sugar together in a bowl and gradually beat in the eggs with the cocoa. Melt the chocolate in a heatproof bowl set over a saucepan of gently simmering water, then beat it into the mixture with the light cream and the chocolate extract.

Reduce the oven temperature to 325°F/160°C. Pour the mixture into the pie shell and bake for 45 minutes, or until the filling has set gently.

Let the mud pie cool completely, then transfer it to a serving plate. Cover with the whipped cream.

Decorate the pie with chocolate flakes and curls and then let chill until ready to serve.

PIE DOUGH

1½ cups all-purpose flour, plus extra for dusting
2 tbsp unsweetened cocoa
generous ½ cup unsalted butter
2 tbsp superfine sugar
1–2 tbsp cold water

FILLING

¾ cup unsalted butter
scant 1¾ cups packed brown sugar
4 eggs, lightly beaten
4 tbsp unsweetened cocoa, sifted
5½ oz/150 g semisweet chocolate
1¼ cups light cream
1 tsp chocolate extract

TO DECORATE

scant 2 cups heavy cream, whipped
chocolate flakes and curls

Chocolate Crumble Pie

SERVES 8

To make the pie dough, sift the flour and baking powder into a large bowl, rub in the butter, and stir in the sugar, then add the egg and a little water to bring the dough together. Turn the dough out, and knead briefly. Wrap the dough in plastic wrap and let chill in the refrigerator for 30 minutes.

Preheat the oven to 375°F/190°C. Roll out the pie dough and use to line a 9-inch/23-cm loose-bottom tart pan. Prick the pastry shell with a fork. Line with parchment paper and fill with dried beans or baking beans. Bake in the oven for 15 minutes. Remove from the oven and take out the paper and beans. Reduce the oven temperature to 350°F/180°C.

To make the filling, bring the cream and milk to a boil in a saucepan, immediately remove from the heat, and add the chocolate. Stir until melted and smooth. Beat the eggs and add to the chocolate mixture, mix thoroughly and pour into the shell. Bake for 15 minutes, remove from the oven, and let rest for 1 hour.

When you are ready to serve the pie, place the topping ingredients in a food processor and pulse to chop. (If you do not have a processor, place the sugar in a large bowl, chop the nuts and chocolate with a large knife, and crush the cookies, then add to the bowl with the cocoa and mix well.) Sprinkle over the pie, then serve it in slices.

PIE DOUGH

scant 1¼ cups all-purpose flour
1 tsp baking powder
½ cup unsalted butter, cut into
   small pieces
¼ cup superfine sugar
1 egg yolk
1–2 tsp cold water

FILLING

⅔ cup heavy cream
⅔ cup milk
8 oz/225 g semisweet chocolate,
   chopped
2 eggs

CRUMBLE TOPPING

generous ½ cup packed
   brown sugar
¾ cup toasted pecans
4 oz/115 g semisweet chocolate
3 oz/85 g amaretti cookies
1 tsp unsweetened cocoa

Chocolate Chiffon Pie

SERVES 8

Preheat the oven to 400°F/200°C. Place the whole Brazil nuts in a food processor and process until finely ground. Add the granulated sugar and melted butter and process briefly to combine. Transfer the mixture into a 9-inch/23-cm round tart pan and press it onto the base and around the sides with a spoon or your fingertips. Bake in the preheated oven for 8–10 minutes, or until light golden brown. Set aside to cool.

For the filling, pour the milk into a heatproof bowl and sprinkle the gelatin over the surface. Let it soften for 2 minutes, then set over a saucepan of gently simmering water. Stir in half of the superfine sugar, both the egg yolks, and all the chocolate. Stir constantly over low heat for 4–5 minutes, until the gelatin has dissolved and the chocolate has melted. Remove from the heat and beat until the mixture is smooth. Stir in the vanilla extract, wrap in plastic wrap, and let chill in the refrigerator for 45–60 minutes until starting to set.

Whip the cream until it is stiff, then fold all but about 3 tablespoons into the chocolate mixture. Whisk the egg whites in a separate, clean, greasefree bowl until soft peaks form. Add 2 teaspoons of the remaining sugar and whisk until stiff peaks form. Fold in the remaining sugar, then fold the egg whites into the chocolate mixture. Pour the filling into the pie shell and let chill in the refrigerator for 3 hours. Decorate the pie with the remaining whipped cream and the whole and chopped Brazil nuts before serving.

PIE SHELL

scant 2 cups shelled Brazil nuts
4 tbsp granulated sugar
4 tsp melted butter

FILLING

1 cup milk
2 tsp powdered gelatin
1/2 cup superfine sugar
2 eggs, separated
8 oz/225 g semisweet chocolate,
  roughly chopped
2/3 cup heavy cream
1 tsp vanilla extract
2 tbsp Brazil nuts, whole and
  chopped, to decorate

Blackberry Chocolate Flan

SERVES 6

To make the pie dough, sift the flour, cocoa, confectioners' sugar, and salt into a mixing bowl and make a well in the center. Place the butter and egg yolk in the well and gradually mix in the dry ingredients, using a dough mixer or two forks. Knead lightly and form into a ball. Wrap the pie dough in plastic wrap and let chill in the refrigerator for 1 hour.

Preheat the oven to 350°F/180°C. Roll out the dough on a lightly floured counter. Use it to line a 12 x 4-inch/30 x 10-cm rectangular flan pan and prick the pie shell with a fork. Line the bottom with parchment paper and fill with dried beans or baking beans. Bake in the preheated oven for 15 minutes. Remove the flan pan, paper, and beans from the oven, and set aside to cool.

To make the filling, place the cream and jelly in a saucepan and bring to a boil over low heat. Remove from the heat and stir in the chocolate and then the butter until melted and smooth. Pour the mixture into the pie shell and set aside to cool.

To make the sauce, put the blackberries, lemon juice, and superfine sugar in a food processor and process until smooth. Strain through a nylon sieve into a bowl and stir in the cassis. Set aside.

Remove the flan from the pan and place on a serving plate. Arrange the remaining blackberries on top and brush with a little blackberry and liqueur sauce. Serve the flan with the remaining sauce on the side.

PIE DOUGH

1 cup all-purpose flour, plus
   extra for dusting
1/4 cup unsweetened cocoa
1/2 cup confectioners' sugar
pinch of salt
6 tbsp unsalted butter, cut into
   small pieces
1/2 egg yolk

FILLING

1 1/4 cups heavy cream
6 oz/175 g blackberry jelly
8 oz/225 g semisweet chocolate,
   broken into pieces
2 tbsp unsalted butter, cut into
   small pieces

SAUCE

1 lb 8 oz/675 g blackberries, plus
   extra for decoration
1 tbsp lemon juice
2 tbsp superfine sugar
2 tbsp crème de cassis

Toffee Chocolate Puff Tarts

MAKES 12

Line the bottoms of a 12-hole nonstick muffin pan with disks of wax paper.

Cut out twelve 2-inch/5-cm circles from the edge of the pie dough and cut the remainder into 12 strips. Roll the strips to half their thickness and line the sides of each hole with 1 strip. Put a disk of pie dough at the bottom, and press well together to seal and make a tart shell. Prick the bottoms and chill in the refrigerator for 30 minutes.

Preheat the oven to 400°F/200°C. While the pie dough is chilling, melt the chocolate in a heatproof bowl set over a saucepan of gently simmering water. Remove the bowl from the heat, cool slightly, then stir in the cream. Beat the sugar and egg yolks together and mix well with the melted chocolate.

Remove the muffin pan from the refrigerator and put a teaspoonful of toffee sauce into each tart shell. Divide the chocolate mixture among the tarts and bake for 20–25 minutes, turning the tray around halfway through the cooking, until just set. Cool the tarts in the muffin pan then remove carefully, leaving behind the wax paper. Serve with whipped cream and a dusting of unsweetened cocoa.

15 oz/375 g prepared puff pastry
5 oz/140 g semisweet chocolate
1¼ cups heavy cream
¼ cup superfine sugar
4 egg yolks

TO SERVE
4 tbsp store-bought toffee sauce
whipped cream
unsweetened cocoa, for dusting

Chocolate Mousse Tart

SERVES 8

To make the tart shell, mix the graham crackers and amaretti cookies with the butter and press well into the bottom of a 9-inch/23-cm springform cake pan. Chill in the refrigerator.

For the topping, melt the semisweet and milk chocolate in a heatproof bowl set over a saucepan of gently simmering water. Cool slightly, then add the egg yolks and mix well.

In a separate bowl, whip the egg whites until they form soft peaks, then add the superfine sugar and whip until stiff.

Fold the chocolate mixture into the egg whites and pour over the tart shell. Chill in the refrigerator for 8 hours or overnight.

When you are ready to serve the tart, unmold it, transfer to a serving dish, and crumble the chocolate flake bars over the top.

3 oz/85 g graham crackers,
   crushed
3 oz/85 g amaretti cookies,
   crushed
5 tbsp unsalted butter, melted

TOPPING
7 oz/200 g semisweet chocolate
4 oz/115 g milk chocolate
3 large eggs, separated
1/4 cup superfine sugar
3 chocolate flake bars,
   to decorate

Black Forest Roulade

SERVES 8–10

Preheat the oven to 375°F/190°C. Lightly oil and line a jelly roll pan with nonstick parchment paper. Break the chocolate into small pieces and place in a heatproof bowl set over a saucepan of gently simmering water. Add the kirsch and heat gently, stirring until the mixture is smooth. Remove from the pan and set aside.

Place the eggs and superfine sugar in a large heatproof bowl and set over the saucepan of gently simmering water. (Alternatively, place in the bowl of a free-standing mixer and use a balloon whip.) Whisk the eggs and sugar until very thick and creamy and the whisk leaves a trail when dragged across the surface. Remove from the heat and whisk in the cooled chocolate.

Spoon into the prepared jelly roll pan, then tap the pan lightly on a counter to smooth the top. Bake in the preheated oven for 20 minutes, or until the top feels firm to the touch. Remove from the oven and immediately invert onto a whole sheet of parchment paper that has been sprinkled with the confectioners' sugar. Lift off the pan and its lining paper, then roll up, encasing the new parchment paper in the roulade. Let stand until cooled.

For the filling, whip the cream until soft peaks form, then stir in the kirsch, reserving 1–2 tablespoons. Unroll the roulade and spread over the cream to within 1/4 inch/5 mm of the edges. Scatter the cherries over the cream. Carefully roll up the roulade again and place on a serving platter.

1 tsp sunflower oil, for oiling
6 oz/175 g semisweet chocolate
2–3 tbsp kirsch or cognac
5 eggs
1 cup superfine sugar
2 tbsp confectioners' sugar, sifted

FILLING

1 1/2 cups heavy cream
1 tbsp kirsch or cognac
12 oz/350 g fresh black cherries,
  pitted, or 14 oz/400 g canned
  sour cherries, drained and pitted

Crispy Chocolate Pie

SERVES 6

Preheat the oven to 325°F/160°C. Grease an 8-inch/20-cm tart pan and line with parchment paper. Whip the egg whites until stiff peaks form. Gently fold in the ground almonds, ground rice, superfine sugar, and almond extract. Spread the mixture over the bottom and sides of the prepared pan. Bake in the preheated oven for 15 minutes.

Meanwhile, put the chocolate in a heatproof bowl set over a saucepan of gently simmering water until melted. Remove from the heat and cool slightly, then beat in the egg yolks, confectioners' sugar, whiskey, and the heavy cream until thoroughly incorporated.

Remove the tart pan from the oven and pour in the chocolate mixture. Cover with foil, return to the oven, and bake at the same temperature for 20–25 minutes, until set. Remove from the oven and let cool completely.

Add the whipped cream to the top and decorate with the marbled chocolate caraque. Serve immediately.

2 tsp unsalted butter, for greasing
2 egg whites
1 cup ground almonds
$^{1}/_{4}$ cup ground rice
$^{2}/_{3}$ cup superfine sugar
$^{1}/_{4}$ tsp almond extract
8 oz/225 g semisweet chocolate, broken into small pieces
4 egg yolks
4 tbsp confectioners' sugar
4 tbsp whiskey
4 tbsp heavy cream

TO DECORATE
$^{2}/_{3}$ cup whipped cream
marbled chocolate caraque

Chocolate Blueberry Tarts

MAKES 10

To make the pie dough, put the flour, unsweetened cocoa, sugar, and salt in a food processor and pulse to mix. Add the butter, pulse again, then add the egg yolk and a little cold water to form a dough. (If you do not have a processor, put the flour, unsweetened cocoa, sugar, and salt in a large bowl, and rub in the butter until the mixture resembles bread crumbs. Add the egg yolk and a little cold water to form a dough.) Cover the pie dough in plastic wrap and chill in the refrigerator for 30 minutes.

Preheat the oven to 350°F/180°C. Remove the pie dough from the refrigerator and roll out. Use to line ten 4-inch/10-cm tart shells. Freeze for 30 minutes, then bake in the oven for 15–20 minutes. Let cool.

Put the blueberries, cassis, and confectioners' sugar in a pan and warm through so the berries become shiny, but do not burst. Let cool.

For the filling, melt the chocolate in a heatproof bowl set over a saucepan of gently simmering water, then cool slightly. Whip the cream until stiff, then fold in the sour cream and cooled chocolate.

Remove the tart shells to a serving plate and divide the chocolate filling among them, smoothing the surface, then top with the blueberries. Dust over or around the tarts with confectioners' sugar.

1½ cups all-purpose flour
¼ cup unsweetened cocoa
¼ cup superfine sugar
pinch of salt
½ cup unsalted butter
1 large egg yolk
1½ cups blueberries
2 tbsp crème de cassis
2 tsp confectioners' sugar,
   sifted, plus extra for dusting

FILLING
5 oz/140 g semisweet chocolate
1 cup heavy cream
⅔ cup sour cream

Cappuccino Soufflé Desserts

SERVES 6

Preheat the oven to 375°F/190°C. Grease and coat the sides of six ¹/4-cup ramekins with superfine sugar and place on a cookie sheet. Put the cream in a saucepan and warm gently. Stir in the espresso granules until dissolved, then add the Kahlúa.

Divide the mixture among the prepared ramekins. Whip the egg whites until soft peaks form, then gradually whisk in the remaining superfine sugar until stiff but not dry. Put the chocolate in a heatproof bowl set over a saucepan of gently simmering water until melted. Add the egg yolks to the melted chocolate, then stir in a little of the whisked egg white.

Gradually fold in the remaining egg white. Divide the mixture among the ramekins. Cook in the preheated oven for 15 minutes, until just set. Dust with unsweetened cocoa and serve at once.

unsalted butter, for greasing
scant ¹/4 cup superfine sugar,
  plus extra for coating
6 tbsp whipping cream
2 tsp instant espresso granules
2 tbsp Kahlúa
3 large eggs, separated, plus
  1 extra egg white
5¹/2 oz/150 g semisweet
  chocolate, broken into pieces
unsweetened cocoa, for dusting

Chocolate & Meringue Dessert

SERVES 4

Preheat the oven to 350°F/180°C. Break the chocolate into small pieces and place in a saucepan with the chocolate-flavored milk. Heat gently, stirring, until the chocolate melts. Bring almost to a boil, then remove the pan from the heat.

Place the bread crumbs in a large mixing bowl with 5 teaspoons of the superfine sugar. Pour over the chocolate milk and mix well. Beat in the egg yolks.

Spoon into a 5-cup pie dish and bake in the preheated oven for 25–30 minutes, or until set and firm to the touch.

Whip the egg whites in a large greasefree bowl until soft peaks form. Gradually whip in the remaining superfine sugar and whip until you have a glossy, thick meringue.

Spread the cherry jelly over the surface of the chocolate mixture and pile the meringue on top. Return the dessert to the oven for about 15 minutes, or until the meringue is crisp and golden.

1¾ oz/50 g semisweet chocolate
2 cups chocolate-flavored milk
1¾ cups fresh white or whole
  wheat bread crumbs
½ cup superfine sugar
2 eggs, separated
4 tbsp cherry jelly

Baked to Perfection

Double Chocolate Muffins

MAKES 12

Preheat the oven to 400°F/200°C. Line a 12-cup muffin pan with paper liners.

Sift the flour, cocoa, baking powder, and cinnamon into a large mixing bowl.

Stir in the sugar and 4¹/₂ oz/125 g of the white chocolate.

Place the eggs and oil in a separate bowl and whisk until frothy, then gradually whisk in the milk. Stir into the dry ingredients until just blended. Divide the batter evenly among the paper liners, filling each three-quarters full. Bake in the oven for 20 minutes, or until well risen and springy to the touch. Remove the muffins from the oven, let cool in the pan for 2 minutes, then remove and place them on a cooling rack to cool completely.

Place the remaining white chocolate in a heatproof bowl, set the bowl over a saucepan of barely simmering water, and heat until melted. Spread over the top of the muffins. Let set, then dust the tops with a little cocoa and serve.

scant 1¹/₂ cups all-purpose flour
¹/₃ cup unsweetened cocoa, plus extra for dusting
1 tbsp baking powder
1 tsp ground cinnamon
¹/₂ cup superfine sugar
6¹/₂ oz/185 g white chocolate, broken into pieces
2 large eggs
¹/₃ cup sunflower oil or peanut oil
1 cup milk

Chocolate Chip Muffins

MAKES 12

Preheat the oven to 400°F/200°C. Line a 12-cup muffin pan with paper liners.

Place the margarine and sugar in a mixing bowl and beat with a wooden spoon until light and fluffy. Beat in the eggs, yogurt, and milk until combined.

Sift the flour and baking soda together and add to the batter. Stir until just blended.

Stir in the chocolate chips, then divide the batter evenly among the paper liners and bake in the oven for 25 minutes, or until risen and golden. Remove the muffins from the oven and let cool in the pan for 5 minutes, then place them on a cooling rack to cool completely.

3 tbsp soft margarine

1 cup superfine sugar

2 large eggs

⅔ cup whole plain yogurt

5 tbsp milk

2 cups all-purpose flour

1 tsp baking soda

1 cup semisweet chocolate chips

Chocolate Orange Muffins

MAKES 8-10

Preheat the oven to 375°F/190°C. Thoroughly oil 10 cups of a 12-cup muffin pan.

Sift both flours into a mixing bowl and stir in the ground almonds and sugar.

Mix the orange zest and juice, cream cheese, and eggs together in a separate bowl. Make a well in the center of the dry ingredients and stir in the wet ingredients, then add the chocolate chips. Beat well to combine all the ingredients.

Divide the batter evenly among the cups, filling each no more than three-quarters full.

Bake in the oven for 20-25 minutes until well risen and golden brown.

Remove from the oven and let cool slightly on a cooling rack, but eat them as fresh as possible.

sunflower oil or peanut oil,
 for oiling
scant 1 cup self-rising white flour
scant 1 cup self-rising whole
 wheat flour
¼ cup ground almonds
¼ cup packed brown sugar
zest and juice of 1 orange
¾ cup cream cheese
2 large eggs
⅓ cup semisweet chocolate chips

Spiced Chocolate Muffins

MAKES 12

Preheat the oven to 375°F/190°C. Line a 12-cup muffin pan with paper liners.

Place the butter, superfine sugar, and brown sugar in a bowl and beat well. Beat in the eggs, sour cream, and milk until thoroughly mixed. Sift the flour, baking soda, cocoa, and allspice into a separate bowl, then stir into the sugar mixture. Add the chocolate chips and mix well. Divide the batter evenly among the paper liners. Bake in the oven for 25–30 minutes.

Remove from the oven and let cool for 10 minutes. Place them on a cooling rack and let cool completely. Store in an airtight container until ready to eat.

3½ oz/100 g unsalted butter, softened

½ cup superfine sugar

½ cup packed brown sugar

2 large eggs

⅔ cup sour cream

5 tbsp milk

1¾ cups all-purpose flour

1 tsp baking soda

2 tbsp unsweetened cocoa

1 tsp allspice

1 cup semisweet chocolate chips

Triple Chocolate Muffins

MAKES 12

Preheat the oven to 400°F/200°C. Line a 12-cup muffin pan with paper liners. Sift the flour, cocoa, baking powder, and baking soda into a large bowl, add the semisweet and white chocolate chips, and stir.

Place the eggs, sour cream, sugar, and melted butter in a separate mixing bowl and mix well. Add the wet ingredients to the dry ingredients and stir gently until just combined.

Using 2 spoons, divide the batter evenly among the paper liners and bake in the preheated oven for 20 minutes, or until well risen and firm to the touch. Remove from the oven and serve warm, or place on a cooling rack and let cool.

1¾ cups all-purpose flour
⅓ cup unsweetened cocoa
2 tsp baking powder
½ tsp baking soda
½ cup semisweet chocolate
  chips
½ cup white chocolate chips
2 large eggs, beaten
1¼ cups sour cream
6 tbsp packed brown sugar
6 tbsp unsalted butter, melted

Mocha Muffins

MAKES 12

Preheat the oven to 375°F/190°C. Oil a 12-cup muffin pan with sunflower oil, or line it with 12 paper liners. Sift the flour, baking powder, cocoa, and salt into a large mixing bowl.

In a separate large bowl, cream the butter and raw brown sugar together, then stir in the beaten egg. Pour in the milk, almond extract, and coffee, then add the coffee powder, chocolate chips, and raisins, and gently mix together. Add the raisin mixture to the flour mixture and then gently stir together until just combined. Do not overstir the batter—it is fine for it to be a little lumpy.

Divide the muffin batter evenly among the 12 cups in the muffin pan or the paper liners (they should be about two-thirds full). To make the topping, place the raw brown sugar in a bowl, add the cocoa and allspice, and mix together well. Sprinkle the topping over the muffins, then transfer to the oven and bake for 20 minutes, or until risen and golden. Remove the muffins from the oven and serve warm, or place them on a cooling rack and let cool.

1 tbsp sunflower oil or peanut
   oil, for oiling
1¾ cups all-purpose flour
1 tbsp baking powder
2 tbsp unsweetened cocoa
pinch of salt
½ cup unsalted butter, melted
scant ¾ cup raw brown sugar
1 large egg, beaten
1 cup milk
1 tsp almond extract
2 tbsp strong coffee
1 tbsp instant coffee powder
¼ cup semisweet chocolate
   chips
scant ⅓ cup raisins

COCOA TOPPING
3 tbsp raw brown sugar
1 tbsp unsweetened cocoa
1 tsp allspice

Marshmallow Muffins

MAKES 12

Preheat the oven to 375°F/190°C. Line a 12-cup muffin pan with paper liners. Melt the butter in a saucepan.

Sift the flour, cocoa, and baking powder together in a large bowl. Stir in the sugar, chocolate chips, and marshmallows until thoroughly mixed.

Whisk the egg, milk, and melted butter together in a separate bowl, then gently stir into the flour to form a stiff batter. Divide the batter evenly among the paper liners.

Bake in the oven for 20-25 minutes until well risen. Remove from the oven and let cool in the pan for 5 minutes, then place on a cooling rack and let cool completely.

5 tbsp unsalted butter

2 cups all-purpose flour

6 tbsp unsweetened cocoa

3 tsp baking powder

6 tbsp superfine sugar

½ cup milk chocolate chips

¼ cup multicolored mini marshmallows

1 large egg, beaten

1¼ cups milk

Chocolate Brownies

MAKES 15

Preheat the oven to 350°F/180°C. Grease and line an 11 x 7-inch/28 x 18-cm rectangular cake pan with parchment paper.

Put the butter and chopped dark chocolate into a heatproof bowl and set over a saucepan of simmering water until melted. Remove from the heat. Sift the flour into a large bowl, add the sugar, and mix well. Stir the eggs into the chocolate mixture, then beat into the flour mixture. Add the nuts, golden raisins, and chocolate chips, and mix well. Spoon evenly into the cake pan and level the surface.

Bake in the oven for 30 minutes, or until firm. To check whether the brownies are cooked through, insert a toothpick into the center—it should come out clean. If not, return the cake to the oven for a few minutes. Remove from the oven and let cool for 15 minutes. Turn out onto a wire rack to cool completely. To decorate, drizzle the melted white chocolate in fine lines over the cake, then cut into bars or squares. Let set before serving.

1 cup unsalted butter, diced, plus extra for greasing
5 1/2 oz/150 g dark chocolate, chopped
1 1/2 cups all-purpose flour
1 cup dark brown sugar
4 eggs, beaten
1/4 cup blanched hazelnuts, chopped
1/2 cup golden raisins
1/2 cup dark chocolate chips
4 oz/115 g white chocolate, melted, to decorate

Double Chocolate Brownies with Fudge Sauce

MAKES 9 LARGE OR 16 SMALL

Preheat the oven to 350°F/180°C. Grease and line a 7-inch/18-cm square cake pan with parchment paper. Place the butter and chocolate in a small heatproof bowl set over a saucepan of gently simmering water until melted. Stir until smooth. Let cool slightly. Stir in the sugar, salt, and vanilla extract. Add the eggs, one at a time, stirring well, until blended.

Sift the flour and unsweetened cocoa into the cake batter and beat until smooth. Stir in the chocolate chips, then pour the batter into the pan. Bake in the preheated oven for 35–40 minutes, or until the top is evenly colored and a skewer inserted into the center comes out almost clean. Let cool slightly while preparing the sauce.

To make the sauce, place the butter, sugar, milk, cream, and corn syrup in a small saucepan and heat gently until the sugar has dissolved. Bring to a boil and stir for 10 minutes, or until the mixture is caramel-colored. Remove from the heat and add the chocolate. Stir until smooth. Cut the brownies into large or small squares and serve immediately with the sauce.

½ cup unsalted butter, plus extra for greasing
4 oz/115 g semisweet chocolate, broken into pieces
1⅓ cups superfine sugar
pinch of salt
1 tsp vanilla extract
2 large eggs
1 cup all-purpose flour
2 tbsp unsweetened cocoa
½ cup white chocolate chips

FUDGE SAUCE
4 tbsp butter
1 cup superfine sugar
⅔ cup milk
1 cup heavy cream
⅔ cup corn syrup
7 oz/200 g semisweet chocolate, broken into pieces

Chocolate Fudge Brownies

MAKES 16

Preheat the oven to 350°F/180°C. Lightly grease an 8-inch/20-cm square shallow cake pan and line with parchment paper.

Beat together the cream cheese, vanilla extract, and 5 teaspoons of superfine sugar until smooth, then set aside.

Beat the eggs and remaining superfine sugar together in a separate bowl until light and fluffy. Place the butter and unsweetened cocoa in a small pan and heat gently, stirring until the butter melts and the mixture combines, then stir it into the egg mixture. Fold in the flour and nuts.

Pour half of the cake batter into the pan and smooth the top. Carefully spread the cream cheese over it, then cover it with the remaining cake batter. Bake in the preheated oven for 40–45 minutes. Let cool in the pan.

To make the frosting, melt the butter in the milk. Stir in the confectioners' sugar and unsweetened cocoa. Spread the frosting over the brownies, and decorate with pecans (if using). Let the frosting set, then cut into bars or squares to serve.

6 tbsp unsalted butter, plus
   extra for greasing
scant 1 cup lowfat cream
   cheese
1/2 tsp vanilla extract
1 cup superfine sugar
2 eggs
3 tbsp unsweetened cocoa
3/4 cup self-rising flour, sifted
1/3 cup chopped pecans

FUDGE FROSTING
4 tbsp butter
1 tbsp milk
2/3 cup confectioners' sugar
2 tbsp unsweetened cocoa
pecans, to decorate (optional)

Sticky Chocolate Brownies

MAKES 9

Preheat the oven to 350°F/180°C. Lightly grease an 8-inch/20-cm shallow square cake pan and line with parchment paper.

Place the butter, sugars, chocolate, and corn syrup in a heavy-bottom saucepan and heat gently, stirring until the mixture is well blended and smooth. Remove from the heat and let cool.

In a separate bowl, beat together the eggs and the chocolate extract or vanilla extract. Whisk in the cooled chocolate mixture.

In another bowl, sift together the flour, unsweetened cocoa, and baking powder, then fold carefully into the egg and chocolate mixture using a metal spoon or spatula.

Spoon the cake batter into the prepared pan and bake in the preheated oven for 25 minutes, until the top is crisp and the edge of the cake is starting to shrink away from the pan. The inside of the cake batter will still be quite heavy and soft to the touch.

Let the cake cool completely in the pan, dust with unsweetened cocoa powder, then cut into squares and serve.

6 tbsp unsalted butter,
 plus extra for greasing
¾ cup superfine sugar
½ cup dark brown sugar
4½ oz/125 g semisweet chocolate
1 tbsp corn syrup
2 eggs
1 tsp chocolate extract or
 vanilla extract
¾ cup all-purpose flour
2 tbsp unsweetened cocoa,
 plus extra to dust
½ tsp baking powder

White Chocolate Brownies

MAKES 9

Preheat the oven to 350°F/180°C. Lightly grease a 7-inch/18-cm square cake pan
and line with parchment paper.

Coarsely chop 6 oz/175 g of the chocolate and all the walnuts. Put the remaining
chocolate and the butter in a heatproof bowl and set over a saucepan of gently
simmering water. When melted, stir together, then set aside to cool slightly.

Whisk the eggs and sugar together, then beat in the cooled chocolate mixture
until well mixed. Fold in the flour, chopped chocolate, and the walnuts. Turn the
mixture into the prepared pan and smooth the surface.

Transfer the pan to the preheated oven and bake the brownies for about
30 minutes, until just set. The mixture should still be a little soft in the center.
Let cool in the pan, then cut into bars or squares before serving.

½ cup unsalted butter, plus
    extra for greasing
8 oz/225 g white chocolate
⅔ cup walnut pieces
2 eggs
1 cup brown sugar
1 cup self-rising flour

Marbled Chocolate Cheesecake Brownies

MAKES 12

Preheat the oven to 350°F/180°C. Grease an 11 x 7-inch/28 x 18-cm cake pan and line with parchment paper.

Melt the butter in a medium saucepan, remove from the heat, and stir in the unsweetened cocoa and the sugar. Beat in the eggs, then add the flour, and stir to mix evenly. Pour into the prepared pan.

For the cheesecake mix, beat together the ricotta, sugar, and egg, then drop teaspoonfuls of the mixture over the chocolate mixture. Use a metal spatula to swirl the two mixtures lightly together.

Bake for 40–45 minutes, until just firm to the touch. Cool in the pan, then cut into bars or squares.

¾ cup unsalted butter, plus
    extra for greasing
3 tbsp unsweetened cocoa
1 cup superfine sugar
2 eggs, beaten
1 cup all-purpose flour

CHEESECAKE MIX
1 cup ricotta cheese
3 tbsp superfine sugar
1 egg, beaten

Black Russian Brownies

MAKES 8–10

Preheat the oven to 350°F/180°C. Grease and line a 12 x 8-inch/30 x 20-cm shallow cake pan with parchment paper.

Melt the chocolate and the butter with the peppercorns in a small saucepan over low heat. Remove from the heat and let cool slightly.

Beat together the eggs, sugar, and vanilla extract in a large bowl and stir in the chocolate mixture, Kahlúa, and vodka.

Sift the flour and baking powder into a separate bowl, then stir evenly into the chocolate mixture. Stir in the walnuts. Pour into the pan and bake for 20–25 minutes, until just firm to the touch.

Let cool for a few minutes, then cut into bars or squares and lift carefully from the pan onto serving plates.

For the topping, stir the Kahlúa into the crème fraîche and spoon a generous mound on each serving of brownie. Dust with a little unsweetened cocoa and serve immediately.

½ cup unsalted butter, plus extra for greasing
4 oz/115 g bittersweet chocolate, broken into pieces
½ tsp coarsely ground black peppercorns
4 eggs, beaten
1¼ cups superfine sugar
1 tsp vanilla extract
3 tbsp Kahlúa liqueur
2 tbsp vodka
1⅓ cups all-purpose flour
¼ tsp baking powder
½ cup chopped walnuts

KAHLUA CREAM TOPPING
2 tbsp Kahlúa liqueur
scant 1 cup crème fraîche or sour cream
unsweetened cocoa, for dusting

Chocolate Butterfly Cakes

MAKES 12

Preheat the oven to 350°F/180°C. Put 12 paper baking cases in a muffin pan, or put 12 double-layer paper cases on a baking sheet.

Put the margarine, sugar, flour, eggs, and cocoa in a large bowl and, using a handheld electric mixer, beat together until just smooth. Beat in the melted chocolate. Spoon the batter into the paper cases, filling them three-quarters full.

Bake the cupcakes in the preheated oven for 15 minutes, or until springy to the touch. Transfer to a wire rack and let cool.

To make the filling, put the butter in a bowl and beat until fluffy. Sift in the confectioners' sugar and beat together until smooth. Add the melted chocolate and beat together until well mixed.

When the cupcakes are cooled, use a serrated knife to cut a circle from the top of each cake and then cut each circle in half. Spread or pipe a little of the buttercream into the center of each cupcake and press the 2 semicircular halves into it at an angle to resemble butterfly wings. Dust with sifted confectioners' sugar before serving.

½ cup soft margarine
½ cup superfine sugar
1½ cups self-rising white flour
2 large eggs
2 tbsp unsweetened cocoa
1 oz/25 g semisweet chocolate,
  melted
confectioners' sugar, for dusting

FILLING

6 tbsp unsalted butter, softened
1½ cups confectioners' sugar
1 oz/25 g semisweet chocolate,
  melted

Dark & White Fudge Cupcakes

MAKES 20

Preheat the oven to 350°F/180°C. Put 20 paper baking cases in 2 muffin pans, or put 20 double-layer paper cases on 2 cookie sheets.

Put the water, butter, superfine sugar, and corn syrup in a saucepan. Heat gently, stirring, until the sugar has dissolved, then bring to a boil. Reduce the heat and cook gently for 5 minutes. Remove from the heat and let cool.

Meanwhile, put the milk and vanilla extract in a bowl. Add the baking soda and stir to dissolve. Sift the flour and cocoa into a separate bowl and add the corn syrup mixture. Stir in the milk and beat until smooth. Spoon the batter into the paper cases until they are two-thirds full.

Bake the cupcakes in the preheated oven for 20 minutes, or until well risen and firm to the touch. Transfer to a wire rack and let cool.

To make the topping, break the semisweet chocolate into a small heatproof bowl, add half the water and half the butter, and set the bowl over a pan of gently simmering water until melted. Stir until smooth and let stand over the water. Using another bowl, repeat with the white chocolate and remaining water and butter. Sift half the sugar into each bowl and beat until smooth and thick. Top the cupcakes with the frostings. Let set. Serve decorated with chocolate shavings.

scant 1 cup water
6 tbsp unsalted butter
6 tbsp superfine sugar
1 tbsp corn syrup
3 tbsp milk
1 tsp vanilla extract
1 tsp baking soda
1½ cups all-purpose flour
2 tbsp unsweetened cocoa

TOPPING

1¾ oz/50 g semisweet chocolate
4 tbsp water
3½ tbsp unsalted butter
1¾ oz/50 g white chocolate
3 cups confectioners' sugar

CHOCOLATE SHAVINGS

3½ oz/100 g semisweet chocolate
3½ oz/100 g white chocolate

Jumbo Chocolate Chip Cupcakes

MAKES 8

Preheat the oven to 375°F/190°C. Put 8 muffin paper cases in a muffin pan.

Put the margarine, sugar, eggs, and flour in a large bowl and, using a handheld electric mixer, beat together until just smooth. Fold in the chocolate chips and spoon the batter into the paper cases.

Bake the cupcakes in the preheated oven for 20–25 minutes, or until well risen and golden brown. Transfer to a wire rack to cool.

scant ½ cup soft margarine
½ cup superfine sugar
2 large eggs
scant ¾ cup self-rising white flour
½ cup semisweet chocolate chips

Chocolate Cupcakes with Cream Cheese Frosting

MAKES 18

Preheat the oven to 400°F/200°C. Put 18 paper baking cases in 2 muffin pans, or put 18 double-layer paper cases on a cookie sheet.

Put the butter and sugar in a bowl and beat together until light and fluffy. Gradually add the eggs, beating well after each addition. Add the milk, then fold in the chocolate chips. Sift in the flour and cocoa, then fold into the mixture. Spoon the batter into the paper cases and smooth the tops.

Bake the cupcakes in the preheated oven for 20 minutes, or until well risen and springy to the touch. Transfer to a wire rack and let cool.

To make the frosting, break the chocolate into a small heatproof bowl and set the bowl over a saucepan of gently simmering water until melted. Let cool slightly. Put the cream cheese in a bowl and beat until softened, then beat in the slightly cooled chocolate.

Spread a little of the frosting over the top of each cupcake, then let chill in the refrigerator for 1 hour before serving. Serve decorated with the chocolate curls.

6 tbsp unsalted butter, softened, or soft margarine
1/2 cup superfine sugar
2 eggs, lightly beaten
2 tbsp milk
1/3 cup semisweet chocolate chips
1 1/2 cups self-rising white flour
1/4 cup unsweetened cocoa

FROSTING

8 oz/225 g white chocolate
2/3 cup lowfat cream cheese
chocolate curls, to decorate

Warm Molten-Centered Chocolate Cupcakes

MAKES 8

Preheat the oven to 375°F/190°C. Put 8 paper baking cases in a muffin pan, or put 8 double-layer paper cases on a cookie sheet.

Put the margarine, sugar, egg, flour, and cocoa in a large bowl and, using a handheld electric mixer, beat together until just smooth.

Spoon half of the batter into the paper cases. Using a teaspoon, make an indentation in the center of each cake. Break the chocolate evenly into 8 squares and place a piece in each indentation, then spoon the remaining cake batter on top.

Bake the cupcakes in the preheated oven for 20 minutes, or until well risen and springy to the touch. Leave the cupcakes for 2-3 minutes before serving warm, dusted with sifted confectioners' sugar.

4 tbsp soft margarine
¼ cup superfine sugar
1 large egg
½ cup self-rising flour
1 tbsp unsweetened cocoa
2 oz/55 g semisweet chocolate
confectioners' sugar, for dusting

Devil's Food Cakes with Chocolate Frosting

MAKES 18

Preheat the oven to 350°F/180°C. Put 18 paper baking cases in a muffin pan, or put 18 double-layer paper cases on a cookie sheet.

Put the margarine, sugar, eggs, flour, baking soda, and cocoa in a large bowl and, using a handheld electric mixer, beat together until just smooth. Using a metal spoon, fold in the sour cream. Spoon the batter into the paper cases.

Bake the cupcakes in the preheated oven for 20 minutes, or until well risen and firm to the touch. Transfer to a wire rack to cool.

To make the frosting, break the chocolate into a heatproof bowl. Set the bowl over a saucepan of gently simmering water and heat until melted, stirring occasionally. Remove from the heat and let cool slightly, then whisk in the sugar and sour cream until combined. Spread the frosting over the tops of the cupcakes and let set in the refrigerator before serving. Serve decorated with chocolate caraque.

3½ tbsp soft margarine
½ cup firmly packed brown sugar
2 large eggs
¾ cup all-purpose flour
½ tsp baking soda
¼ cup unsweetened cocoa
½ cup sour cream

FROSTING
4½ oz/125 g semisweet chocolate
2 tbsp superfine sugar
⅔ cup sour cream
chocolate caraque, to decorate

Mocha Cupcakes with Whipped Cream

MAKES 20

Preheat the oven to 350°F/180°C. Put 20 paper baking cases in 2 muffin pans, or put 20 double-layer paper cases on 2 cookie sheets.

Put the coffee powder, butter, sugar, honey, and water in a saucepan and heat gently, stirring, until the sugar has dissolved. Bring to a boil, then reduce the heat and let simmer for 5 minutes. Pour into a large heatproof bowl and let cool.

When the mixture has cooled, sift in the flour and cocoa. Dissolve the baking soda in the milk, then add to the mixture with the egg and beat together until smooth. Spoon the batter into the paper cases.

Bake the cupcakes in the preheated oven for 15–20 minutes, or until well risen and firm to the touch. Transfer to a wire rack to cool.

For the topping, whip the cream in a bowl until it holds its shape. Just before serving, spoon heaping teaspoonfuls of cream on top of each cake, then dust lightly with sifted cocoa. Store the cupcakes in the refrigerator until ready to serve.

2 tbsp instant espresso coffee powder
6 tbsp unsalted butter
6 tbsp superfine sugar
1 tbsp honey
scant 1 cup water
1½ cups all-purpose flour
2 tbsp unsweetened cocoa
1 tsp baking soda
3 tbsp milk
1 large egg, lightly beaten

TOPPING
1 cup whipping cream
unsweetened cocoa, sifted, for dusting

Tiny Chocolate Cupcakes with Ganache Frosting

MAKES 20

Preheat the oven to 375°F/190°C. Put 20 double-layer mini paper cases on 2 cookie sheets.

Put the butter and sugar in a bowl and beat together until light and fluffy. Gradually beat in the egg. Sift in the flour and cocoa and then, using a metal spoon, fold them into the mixture. Stir in the milk.

Take a pastry bag fitted with a large plain tip, fill it with the batter, and pipe it into the paper cases, filling each one until half full.

Bake the cakes in the preheated oven for 10–15 minutes, or until well risen and firm to the touch. Transfer to a wire rack to cool.

To make the frosting, break the chocolate into a pan and add the cream. Heat gently, stirring all the time, until the chocolate has melted. Pour into a large heatproof bowl and, using a handheld electric mixer, beat the mixture for 10 minutes, or until thick, glossy, and cool.

Take a pastry bag fitted with a large star tip, fill it with the frosting, and pipe a swirl on top of each cupcake. Alternatively, spoon the frosting over the top of each cupcake. Chill in the refrigerator for 1 hour before serving. Serve decorated with a chocolate-coated coffee bean (if using).

4 tbsp unsalted butter, softened
1/4 cup superfine sugar
1 large egg, lightly beaten
scant 1/2 cup white self-rising flour
2 tbsp unsweetened cocoa
1 tbsp milk
20 chocolate-coated coffee beans, to decorate (optional)

FROSTING
3 1/2 oz/100 g semisweet chocolate
1/3 cup heavy cream

Crumbly Cookies & Heavenly Bites

Chocolate Chip Oatmeal Cookies

MAKES 20

Preheat the oven to 350°F/180°C. Grease 2 large cookie sheets. Place the butter and sugar in a bowl and beat together with a wooden spoon until light and fluffy.

Beat in the egg, then add the rolled oats, milk, and vanilla extract. Beat together until well blended. Sift the flour, cocoa, and baking powder together and stir into the mixture. Stir in the chocolate pieces.

Place dessertspoonfuls of the mixture on the prepared cookie sheets and flatten slightly with a fork. Bake in the preheated oven for 15 minutes, or until slightly risen and firm. Remove from the oven and cool on the cookie sheets for 2 minutes, then transfer to cooling racks to cool completely.

½ cup unsalted butter, softened, plus extra for greasing
½ cup light brown sugar
1 egg
⅔ cup rolled oats
1 tbsp milk
1 tsp vanilla extract
scant 1 cup all-purpose flour
1 tbsp unsweetened cocoa
½ tsp baking powder
6 squares bittersweet chocolate, broken into pieces
6 squares milk chocolate, broken into pieces

Double Chocolate Chip Cookies

MAKES 24

Preheat the oven to 350°F/180°C, then grease 3 cookie sheets. Place the butter, granulated sugar, and brown sugar in a bowl and beat until light and fluffy. Gradually beat in the egg and vanilla extract.

Sift the flour, cocoa, and baking soda into the mixture and stir in carefully. Stir in the chocolate chips and walnuts. Drop dessertspoonfuls of the mixture onto the prepared cookie sheets, spaced well apart to allow for spreading.

Bake in the oven for 10–15 minutes, or until the mixture has spread and the cookies are beginning to feel firm. Remove from the oven and let cool on the cookie sheets for 2 minutes, before transferring to cooling racks.

1/2 cup unsalted butter, softened, plus extra for greasing
1/4 cup granulated sugar
1/4 cup light brown sugar
1 egg, beaten
1/2 tsp vanilla extract
3/4 cup all-purpose flour
2 tbsp unsweetened cocoa
1/2 tsp baking soda
2/3 cup milk chocolate chips
1/2 cup walnuts, coarsely chopped

Black & White Cookies

MAKES 18–20

Melt the bittersweet chocolate in a heatproof bowl set over a saucepan of gently simmering water. Remove from the heat and let cool. Sift the flour and baking powder together.

Meanwhile, in a large bowl, whisk the egg, sugar, oil, and vanilla extract together. Whisk in the cooled, melted chocolate until well blended, then gradually stir in the flour. Cover the bowl with plastic wrap and chill in the refrigerator for at least 3 hours.

Preheat the oven to 375°F/190°C. Oil 1–2 large cookie sheets. Shape tablespoonfuls of the mixture into log shapes using your hands, each measuring about 2 inches/5 cm. Roll the logs generously in the confectioners' sugar, then place on the prepared cookie sheets, allowing room for the cookies to spread during cooking.

Bake the cookies in the preheated oven for 15 minutes, or until firm. Remove from the oven, and place 3 chocolate buttons down the center of each, alternating the colors. Transfer to a cooling rack and let cool.

2 squares bittersweet chocolate, broken into pieces
1 cup all-purpose flour
1 tsp baking powder
1 egg
scant ¾ cup superfine sugar
scant ¼ cup corn oil, plus extra for oiling
½ tsp vanilla extract
2 tbsp confectioners' sugar
1 small package milk chocolate buttons (about 30 buttons)
1 small package white chocolate buttons (about 30 buttons)

Chocolate Orange Cookies

MAKES 30

Preheat the oven to 350°F/180°C. Line 2 cookie sheets with sheets of parchment paper.

Beat together the butter and sugar until light and fluffy. Beat in the egg and milk until well combined. Sift the flour and unsweetened cocoa into the bowl and gradually mix together to form a soft dough. Use your fingers to incorporate the last of the flour and bring the dough together.

Roll out the dough on a lightly floured counter until 1/4 inch/5 mm thick. Cut out circles using a 2-inch/5-cm fluted round cookie cutter.

Place the circles on the cookie sheets and bake in the oven for 10–12 minutes, or until golden.

Let the cookies cool on the cookie sheet for a few minutes before transferring them to a wire rack to cool completely and become crisp.

To make the frosting, put the confectioners' sugar in a bowl and stir in enough orange juice to form a thin frosting that will coat the back of the spoon. Put a spoonful of frosting in the center of each cookie and let set. Place the semisweet chocolate in a heatproof bowl set over a saucepan of gently simmering water and stir until melted. Drizzle thin lines of melted chocolate over the cookies and let set before serving.

generous 6 tbsp unsalted butter, softened
1/3 cup superfine sugar
1 egg
1 tbsp milk
2 cups all-purpose flour, plus extra for dusting
2 tbsp unsweetened cocoa

FROSTING

1 1/2 cups confectioners' sugar, sifted
3 tbsp orange juice
a little semisweet chocolate, broken into pieces

Nutty Drizzles

MAKES 24

Preheat the oven to 350°F/180°C. Grease 2 large cookie sheets. In a large bowl, cream together the butter, sugar, and egg. Add the flour, baking powder, baking soda, oats, bran, and wheat germ, and mix together until well combined. Finally, stir in the nuts, chocolate chips, and raisins.

Put 24 rounded tablespoonfuls of the mixture onto the prepared cookie sheets. Transfer to the preheated oven and bake for 12 minutes, or until the cookies are golden brown.

Remove the cookies from the oven, then transfer to a cooling rack and let cool. Meanwhile, heat the chocolate pieces in a heatproof bowl set over a saucepan of gently simmering water until melted. Stir the chocolate, then let cool slightly. Use a spoon to drizzle the chocolate in waves over the cookies, or spoon it into a pastry bag and pipe zigzag lines over the cookies. When the chocolate has set, store the cookies in an airtight container in the refrigerator until ready to serve.

generous ¾ cup unsalted butter, plus extra for greasing
scant 1½ cups raw brown sugar
1 egg
scant 1 cup all-purpose flour, sifted
1 tsp baking powder
1 tsp baking soda
1 cup rolled oats
1 tbsp bran
1 tbsp wheat germ
4 oz/115 g mixed nuts, toasted and coarsely chopped
1 cup bittersweet chocolate chips
¾ cup raisins and golden raisins
6 squares semisweet chocolate, coarsely chopped

Cookies & Cream Sandwiches

SERVES 4

Preheat the oven to 325°F/160°C. Line a cookie sheet with nonstick parchment paper. Place the butter and sugar in a large bowl and beat together until light and fluffy. Sift the flour, unsweetened cocoa, and ground cinnamon into the bowl and mix to form a dough.

Place the dough between 2 sheets of nonstick parchment paper and roll out to ¹/₈ inch/3 mm thick. Cut out 2¹/₂-inch/6-cm circles and place on the prepared cookie sheet. Bake in the oven for 15 minutes or until firm to the touch. Let cool for 2 minutes, then transfer to wire racks to cool completely.

Meanwhile, make the filling. Place the chocolate and cream in a pan and heat gently until the chocolate has melted. Stir until smooth. Let cool, then let chill in the refrigerator for 2 hours, or until firm. Sandwich the cookies together in pairs, each with a spoonful of chocolate cream, and serve dusted with the cocoa.

generous ¹/₂ cup unsalted
butter, softened
scant ³/₄ cup confectioners'
sugar
scant 1 cup all-purpose flour
6 tbsp unsweetened cocoa, plus
extra for dusting
¹/₂ tsp ground cinnamon

FILLING
4¹/₂ oz/125 g semisweet
chocolate, broken into pieces
¹/₄ cup heavy cream

White Chocolate Cookies

MAKES 24

Preheat the oven to 375°F/190°C. Grease several cookie sheets lightly with a little butter. In a large mixing bowl, cream together the butter and sugar until light and fluffy.

Gradually add the beaten egg to the creamed mixture, beating well after each addition.

Sift the flour and salt into the creamed mixture and blend well.

Stir in the white chocolate chunks and the chopped Brazil nuts.

Place heaping teaspoonfuls of the dough on the prepared cookie sheets. Put no more than 6 on each sheet because the cookies will spread during cooking.

Bake in the oven for 10–12 minutes, or until just golden brown.

Transfer the cookies to wire racks and let stand until completely cooled.

½ cup unsalted butter, softened, plus extra for greasing
⅔ cup brown sugar
1 egg, beaten
1¾ cups self-rising flour
pinch of salt
4½ oz/125 g white chocolate, chopped
⅓ cup chopped Brazil nuts

Chocolate & Coffee Whole Wheat Cookies

MAKES 24

Preheat the oven to 375°F/190°C. Grease 2 large cookie sheets. Cream the butter and sugar together in a bowl. Add the egg and beat well, using a handheld electric mixer if you prefer.

In a separate bowl, sift together the all-purpose flour, baking soda, and salt, then add in the whole wheat flour and bran. Mix in the egg mixture, then stir in the chocolate chips, oats, coffee, and hazelnuts. Mix well, with a handheld electric mixer if you prefer.

Put 24 rounded tablespoonfuls of the mixture onto the prepared cookie sheets, leaving room for the cookies to spread during cooking. Alternatively, with lightly floured hands, break off pieces of the mixture and roll into balls (about 1 oz/ 25 g each), then place on the cookie sheets and flatten them with the back of a teaspoon. Transfer the cookie sheets to the preheated oven and bake for 16–18 minutes, or until the cookies are golden brown.

Remove from the oven, then transfer to a cooling rack and let cool before serving.

¾ cup unsalted butter or margarine, plus extra for greasing
1 cup brown sugar
1 egg
½ cup all-purpose flour
1 tsp baking soda
pinch of salt
scant ½ cup whole wheat flour
1 tbsp bran
1⅓ cups semisweet chocolate chips
2 cups rolled oats
1 tbsp strong coffee
⅔ cup hazelnuts, toasted and coarsely chopped

Mocha Walnut Cookies

MAKES ABOUT 16

Preheat the oven to 350°F/180°C. Grease 2 cookie sheets. Put the butter, light brown sugar, and granulated sugar in a bowl and beat until light and fluffy. Put the vanilla extract, coffee, and egg in a separate bowl and whisk together.

Gradually add to the butter and sugar, beating until fluffy. Sift the flour, baking powder, and baking soda into the mixture and fold in carefully. Fold in the chocolate chips and chopped walnuts.

Spoon heaping teaspoonfuls of the cookie dough onto the prepared cookie sheets, allowing room for the cookies to spread. Bake for 10–15 minutes, until crisp on the outside but still soft inside. Let cool on the cookie sheets for 2 minutes, then transfer to wire racks to cool completely.

$\frac{1}{2}$ cup unsalted butter, softened, plus extra for greasing

generous $\frac{1}{2}$ cup light brown sugar

scant $\frac{1}{2}$ cup granulated sugar

1 tsp vanilla extract

1 tbsp instant coffee granules dissolved in 1 tbsp hot water

1 egg

$1\frac{1}{2}$ cups all-purpose flour

$\frac{1}{2}$ tsp baking powder

$\frac{1}{4}$ tsp baking soda

scant $\frac{1}{2}$ cup milk chocolate chips

$\frac{1}{2}$ cup walnuts, coarsely chopped

Chocolate Peanut Butter Slices

MAKES 26

Preheat the oven to 350°F/180°C. Finely chop the chocolate. Sift the flour and baking powder into a large bowl.

Add the butter to the flour and rub in until the mixture resembles bread crumbs. Stir in the sugar, oats, and chopped nuts.

Put a quarter of the mixture into a bowl and stir in the chopped chocolate. Set aside.

Stir the egg into the remaining mixture, then press into the bottom of a 12 x 8-inch/ 30 x 20-cm roasting pan.

Bake the bottom layer in the preheated oven for 15 minutes. Meanwhile, mix the condensed milk and peanut butter together. Pour the mixture over the bottom layer and spread evenly, then sprinkle the reserved chocolate mixture on top and press down lightly.

Return to the oven and bake for an additional 20 minutes, until golden brown. Let cool in the pan, then cut into slices.

10½ oz/300 g milk chocolate
2½ cups all-purpose flour
1 tsp baking powder
1 cup unsalted butter
1¾ cups brown sugar
2 cups rolled oats
½ cup chopped mixed nuts
1 egg, beaten
scant 1¾ cups condensed milk
⅓ cup crunchy peanut butter

Chocolate Whole Wheat Cookies

MAKES 20

Preheat the oven to 350°F/180°C. Grease 1–2 cookie sheets. Beat the butter and sugar together in a bowl until fluffy. Add the egg and beat well. Stir in the wheat germ and flours. Bring the mixture together with your hands.

Roll rounded teaspoons of the mixture into balls and place on the prepared cookie sheet or sheets, spaced well apart to allow for spreading. Flatten the cookies slightly with a fork, then bake in the preheated oven for 15–20 minutes, or until golden.

Remove from the oven and let cool on the cookie sheets for a few minutes before transferring to a cooling rack to cool completely.

Melt the chocolate in a heatproof bowl set over a saucepan of gently simmering water, then dip each cookie in the chocolate to cover the bottom and a little way up the sides. Let the excess chocolate drip back into the bowl. Place the cookies on a sheet of parchment paper and let set in a cool place before serving.

6 tbsp unsalted butter, plus extra for greasing

½ cup raw brown sugar

1 egg

scant ¼ cup wheat germ

¾ cup whole wheat self-rising flour

6 tbsp white self-rising flour, sifted

4½ squares semisweet chocolate, broken into pieces

Chocolate Temptations

MAKES 24

Preheat the oven to 350°F/180°C. Grease 1-2 large cookie sheets. Put 8 squares of the bittersweet chocolate with the butter and coffee into a heatproof bowl set over a saucepan of gently simmering water and heat until the chocolate is almost melted.

Meanwhile, beat the eggs in a bowl until fluffy. Gradually whisk in the sugar until thick. Remove the chocolate from the heat and stir until smooth. Add to the egg mixture and stir until combined.

Sift the flour, baking powder, and salt into a bowl, then stir into the chocolate mixture. Chop 3 squares of the remaining bittersweet chocolate into pieces and stir into the mixture. Stir in the almond extract and chopped nuts.

Put 24 tablespoonfuls of the mixture onto the cookie sheet or sheets, then transfer to the preheated oven and bake for 15 minutes. Remove from the oven and transfer to a cooling rack to cool. To decorate, melt the remaining chocolate (bittersweet and white) in turn as earlier, then spoon into a pastry bag and pipe thin lines onto the cookies, alternating the colors.

³⁄₄ cup unsalted butter, plus
  extra for greasing
12¹⁄₂ squares bittersweet
  chocolate
1 tsp strong coffee
2 eggs
scant ³⁄₄ cup soft brown sugar
scant 1¹⁄₄ cups all-purpose flour
¹⁄₄ tsp baking powder
pinch of salt
2 tsp almond extract
¹⁄₂ cup chopped Brazil nuts
¹⁄₂ cup chopped hazelnuts
1¹⁄₂ squares white chocolate

Chocolate Scones

MAKES 4

Preheat the oven to 425°F/220°C. Lightly grease a cookie sheet. Place the flour in a mixing bowl. Cut the butter into small pieces and rub it into the flour with your fingertips until the mixture resembles fine bread crumbs.

Stir in the superfine sugar and chocolate chips, then mix in enough of the milk to form a soft dough.

On a lightly floured counter, roll out the dough to form a 4 x 6-inch/10 x 15-cm rectangle, about 1 inch/2.5 cm thick. Cut the dough into 9 squares.

Place the scones spaced well apart on the prepared cookie sheet.

Brush the tops with a little milk and bake in the preheated oven for 10–12 minutes, until risen and golden.

5 tbsp unsalted butter,
   plus extra for greasing
2 cups self-rising flour, sifted
1 tbsp superfine sugar
⅓ cup chocolate chips
about ⅔ cup milk, plus extra for
   brushing
all-purpose flour, for dusting

Chocolate Pistachio Bars

MAKES 24

Preheat the oven to 325°F/160°C. Grease a cookie sheet with butter. Put the chocolate and butter in a heatproof bowl set over a saucepan of gently simmering water. Stir over low heat until melted and smooth. Remove from the heat and cool slightly.

Sift the flour and baking powder into a bowl and mix in the superfine sugar, cornmeal, lemon zest, amaretto, egg, and pistachios. Stir in the chocolate mixture and mix to a soft dough.

Lightly dust your hands with flour, divide the dough in half, and shape each piece into an 11-inch/28-cm long cylinder. Transfer the cylinders to the prepared cookie sheet and flatten, with the palm of your hand, to about 3/4 inch/2 cm thick. Bake the cookies in the preheated oven for about 20 minutes, until firm to the touch.

Remove the cookie sheet from the oven and let the cooked pieces cool. When cool, put the cooked pieces on a cutting board and slice them diagonally into thin cookies. Return them to the cookie sheet and bake for an additional 10 minutes, until crisp. Remove from the oven, and transfer to a wire rack to cool. Dust lightly with confectioners' sugar.

2 tbsp unsalted butter, plus extra for greasing
6 oz/175 g semisweet chocolate, broken into pieces
2½ cups self-rising flour, plus extra for dusting
1½ tsp baking powder
scant ½ cup superfine sugar
½ cup cornmeal
finely grated zest of 1 lemon
2 tsp amaretto
1 egg, lightly beaten
¾ cup coarsely chopped pistachios
2 tbsp confectioners' sugar, for dusting

Chocolate Caramel Squares

MAKES 16

Preheat the oven to 350°F/180°C. Beat together the margarine and brown sugar in a bowl until light and fluffy. Beat in the flour and the rolled oats. Use your fingertips to bring the mixture together, if necessary.

Press the mixture into the bottom of a shallow 8-inch/20-cm square cake pan.

Bake the mixture in the preheated oven for 25 minutes, or until just golden and firm. Cool in the pan.

Place the ingredients for the caramel filling in a saucepan and heat gently, stirring until the sugar has dissolved. Bring slowly to a boil over very low heat, then boil very gently for 3–4 minutes, stirring constantly, until thickened.

Pour the caramel filling over the oat layer in the pan and let set.

For the topping, melt the semisweet chocolate and spread it over the caramel. If using the white chocolate, place it in a heatproof bowl set over a saucepan of gently simmering water until melted. Pipe lines of white chocolate over the semisweet chocolate. Using a toothpick, feather the white chocolate into the semisweet chocolate. Let set, then cut into squares to serve.

$^{1}/_{3}$ cup soft margarine
$^{1}/_{3}$ cup brown sugar
1 cup all-purpose flour
$^{1}/_{2}$ cup rolled oats

CARAMEL FILLING
2 tbsp unsalted butter
2 tbsp brown sugar
$^{3}/_{4}$ cup condensed milk

TOPPING
3$^{1}/_{2}$ oz/100 g semisweet chocolate
1 oz/25 g white chocolate (optional)

Chocolate Chip Bars

MAKES 12

Preheat the oven to 350°F/180°C. Lightly grease a shallow 8-inch/20-cm square cake pan.

Place the butter, superfine sugar, and corn syrup in a saucepan and cook over low heat, stirring constantly, until the butter and sugar melt and the mixture is well combined.

Remove the pan from the heat and stir in the rolled oats until they are well coated. Add the chocolate chips and the golden raisins and mix well to combine everything.

Turn into the prepared pan and press down well.

Bake in the preheated oven for 30 minutes. Cool slightly, then gently use a knife to mark into bars. When almost cooled cut into bars or squares and transfer to a wire rack to cool completely.

½ cup unsalted butter, plus
 extra for greasing
⅓ cup superfine sugar
1 tbsp corn syrup
4 cups rolled oats
½ cup semisweet chocolate chips
⅓ cup golden raisins

Cookie Sandwiches

MAKES 20

Line 3 cookie sheets with parchment paper, or use 3 nonstick sheets. Cream the butter and sugar together until pale and fluffy. Beat in the egg yolk, then beat in the almonds and flour. Continue beating until thoroughly mixed. Shape the dough into a ball, wrap in plastic wrap, and chill in the refrigerator for 1½–2 hours.

Preheat the oven to 325°F/160°C. Unwrap the dough, break off walnut-size pieces, and roll them into balls between the palms of your hands. Place the dough balls on the prepared cookie sheets, allowing space for the cookies to spread during cooking. You may need to cook them in batches. Bake in the preheated oven for 20–25 minutes, until golden. Carefully transfer the cookies, still on the parchment paper (if using), to wire racks to cool.

Melt the chocolate in a heatproof bowl set over a saucepan of gently simmering water. Remove the cookies from the parchment paper (if using). Spread the melted chocolate on the flat sides and sandwich them together in pairs. Return to the wire racks to cool.

2 cups unsalted butter, sweet
    for preference
½ cup superfine sugar
1 egg yolk
1 cup ground almonds
1¼ cups all-purpose flour
2 oz/55 g semisweet chocolate,
    broken into pieces

Cool Chocolate

Chocolate Chip Ice Cream with Hot Chocolate Fudge Sauce

SERVES 4–6

Pour the milk into a heavy-bottom saucepan, add the vanilla bean, and bring almost to a boil. Remove from the heat and let infuse for 30 minutes. Meanwhile, chop the chocolate into small pieces and set aside.

Put the sugar and egg yolks in a large bowl and whisk together until pale and the mixture leaves a trail when the whisk is lifted. Remove the vanilla bean from the milk, then slowly add the milk to the sugar mixture, stirring all the time with a wooden spoon. Strain the mixture into the rinsed-out saucepan or a double boiler and cook over low heat for 10–15 minutes, stirring all the time, until the mixture thickens enough to coat the back of the spoon. Do not boil or it will curdle.

Remove the custard from the heat and let cool for at least 1 hour, stirring from time to time to prevent a skin from forming. Meanwhile, whip the cream until it holds its shape. Keep in the refrigerator until ready to use.

If using an ice-cream machine, fold the cold custard into the whipped cream, then churn the mixture in the machine following the manufacturer's instructions. Just before the ice cream freezes, add the chocolate pieces. Alternatively, freeze the custard in a freezerproof container, uncovered, for 1–2 hours, or until it starts to set around the edges. Turn the custard into a bowl and stir with a fork or beat in a food processor until smooth. Fold in the whipped cream and chocolate pieces. Return to the freezer and freeze for an additional 2–3 hours, or until firm or ready to serve. Cover the container with a lid for storing.

Make the chocolate sauce just before you serve the ice cream. Put the chocolate, butter, and milk in a heatproof bowl set over a saucepan of simmering water and heat gently, stirring occasionally, until the chocolate has melted and the sauce is smooth. Transfer the mixture to a heavy-bottom saucepan and stir in the sugar and corn syrup. Heat gently until the sugar has dissolved, then bring to a boil. Boil, without stirring, for 5 minutes. Serve the hot sauce poured over the ice cream.

1¼ cups whole milk
1 vanilla bean
4 oz/115 g milk chocolate
scant ½ cup sugar
3 egg yolks
1¼ cups heavy whipping cream
4½ oz/125 g chocolate chips

CHOCOLATE FUDGE SAUCE
1¾ oz/50 g milk chocolate, broken into pieces
2 tbsp unsalted butter
4 tbsp whole milk
1 cup brown sugar
2 tbsp corn syrup

Chocolate Praline Ice Cream

SERVES 4–6

To prepare the praline, brush a cookie sheet with oil. Put the sugar, water, and nuts in a large heavy-bottom saucepan and heat gently, stirring, until the sugar has dissolved, then let the mixture bubble gently for 6–10 minutes, or until lightly golden brown. Do not stir the mixture while it is bubbling and make sure that it does not burn. As soon as the mixture has turned golden brown, immediately pour it onto the prepared cookie sheet and spread it out evenly. Let cool for 1 hour, or until cooled and hardened. When the praline has hardened, finely crush it in a food processor or place it in a plastic bag and crush with a hammer.

To prepare the ice cream, put the chocolate and milk in a saucepan and heat gently, stirring, until the chocolate has melted and the mixture is smooth. Remove from the heat.

Put the sugar and egg yolks in a large bowl and whisk together until pale and the mixture leaves a trail when the whisk is lifted. Slowly add the milk mixture, stirring all the time with a wooden spoon. Strain the mixture into the rinsed-out saucepan or a double boiler and cook over low heat for 10–15 minutes, stirring all the time, until the mixture thickens enough to coat the back of the spoon. Do not let the mixture boil or it will curdle.

Remove the custard from the heat and let cool for at least 1 hour, stirring from time to time to prevent a skin from forming. Meanwhile, whip the cream until it holds its shape. Keep in the refrigerator until ready to use. If using an ice-cream machine, fold the cold custard into the whipped cream, then churn the mixture in the machine following the manufacturer's instructions. Just before the ice cream freezes, add the praline. Alternatively, freeze the custard in a freezerproof container, uncovered, for 1–2 hours, or until it starts to set around the edges. Turn the custard into a bowl and stir with a fork or beat in a food processor until smooth. Fold in the whipped cream and praline. Return to the freezer and freeze for an additional 2–3 hours, or until firm or ready to serve.

3 oz/85 g semisweet chocolate,
  broken into pieces
1¼ cups whole milk
scant ½ cup superfine sugar
3 egg yolks
1¼ cups heavy whipping cream

PRALINE
vegetable oil, for oiling
½ cup granulated sugar
2 tbsp water
scant ⅓ cup blanched almonds

White & Dark Chocolate Ice Cream

SERVES 4

Put the egg yolks and sugar into a large, heatproof bowl and beat until fluffy.
Heat the milk, cream, and dark chocolate in a saucepan over low heat, stirring,
until melted and almost boiling. Remove from the heat and whisk into the egg
mixture. Return to the saucepan and cook, stirring, over low heat until thick.
Do not let it simmer. Transfer to a heatproof bowl and let cool. Cover the bowl
with plastic wrap and chill for 1¹/₂ hours. Remove from the refrigerator and stir
in the white chocolate.

Transfer to a freezerproof container and freeze for 1 hour. Remove from the
freezer, transfer to a bowl, and whisk to break up the ice crystals. Return to the
container and freeze for 30 minutes. Repeat twice more, freezing for 30 minutes
and whisking each time. Alternatively, transfer the mixture to an ice-cream
machine and process for 15 minutes.

Scoop into serving bowls, decorate with mint leaves, and serve.

6 egg yolks
¹/₂ cup superfine sugar
1¹/₂ cups milk
³/₄ cup heavy cream
3¹/₂ oz/100 g dark chocolate,
    chopped
3 oz/85 g white chocolate,
    grated or finely chopped
fresh mint leaves, to decorate

Chocolate Peppermint Crisp Terrine

SERVES 6–8

Line a 1-lb/450-g loaf pan or a 3^1/2-cup oblong freezerproof plastic container with wax paper, allowing it to hang over the edges of the container so that the ice cream can be easily removed. Pour the light cream into a heavy-bottom saucepan and bring almost to a boil. Remove from the heat and stir in the peppermint extract.

Put the egg yolks and sugar in a large bowl and whisk together until pale and the mixture leaves a trail when the whisk is lifted. Slowly add the cream, stirring all the time with a wooden spoon.

Strain the mixture into the rinsed-out saucepan or a double boiler and cook over low heat for 10–15 minutes, stirring all the time, until the mixture thickens enough to coat the back of the spoon. Do not let the mixture boil or it will curdle. Remove the custard from the heat and let cool for at least 1 hour, stirring from time to time to prevent a skin from forming.

Meanwhile, put the peppermint crisps, a few at a time, into a food processor and chop into small pieces. Alternatively, chop the peppermint crisps into small pieces by hand.

Whip the heavy cream until it just holds its shape. When the custard is cold, stir in the peppermint crisp pieces, then fold in the whipped cream until well blended.

Turn the mixture into the prepared pan or plastic container and then freeze, uncovered, for 4 hours, or until firm or ready to serve. To serve the ice cream, uncover, stand the pan or plastic container in hot water for a few seconds to loosen it, then invert it onto a serving dish. Remove the wax paper and, using a hot knife, cut the terrine into slices. Serve decorated with chocolate shapes.

1^1/4 cups light cream
^{1}/2 tsp peppermint extract
4 egg yolks
^{1}/2 cup superfine sugar
7 oz/200 g semisweet chocolate peppermint crisps
1^1/4 cups heavy cream
chocolate shapes, to decorate

Chocolate Ice Cream Roll

SERVES 8

Line a 15-10-inch/38-25-cm jelly roll pan with wax paper. Grease the bottom and dust with flour. Put the eggs and superfine sugar in a heatproof bowl set over a pan of gently simmering water. Whisk over low heat for 5–10 minutes until the mixture is pale and fluffy. Remove from the heat and continue beating for 10 minutes until the mixture is cool and the whisk leaves a ribbon trail when lifted. Sift the flour and unsweetened cocoa over the surface and gently fold in.

Preheat the oven to 375°F/190°C. Pour the mixture into the prepared pan and spread out evenly with a spatula. Bake in the preheated oven for 15 minutes, until firm to the touch and starting to shrink from the sides of the pan.

Spread out a clean dish towel and cover with a sheet of parchment paper. Lightly dust the parchment paper with confectioners' sugar. Turn out the cake onto the parchment paper and carefully peel off the lining paper. Trim off any crusty edges. Starting from a short side, pick up the cake and the parchment paper and roll them up together. Wrap the dish towel around the rolled cake and place on a wire rack to cool.

Remove the ice cream from the freezer and put it in the refrigerator for 15–20 minutes to soften slightly. Remove the dish towel and unroll the cake. Spread the ice cream evenly over the cake, then roll it up again, this time without the parchment paper. Wrap the cake in foil and place in the freezer. Remove the cake from the freezer about 20 minutes before serving. Unwrap, place on a serving plate, and dust with confectioners' sugar. Arrange the chocolate caraque over the top. Place the cake in the refrigerator until ready to serve.

unsalted butter, for greasing
¾ cup all-purpose flour, plus
  extra for dusting
4 eggs
½ cup superfine sugar
3 tbsp unsweetened cocoa
confectioners' sugar, for dusting
2½ cups chocolate ice cream
marbled chocolate caraque,
  to decorate

Chocolate Ice Cream Bombe

SERVES 4

Put a 6¼-cup bombe mold into the freezer and turn the freezer to its lowest setting. Place the eggs, egg yolks, and sugar in a heatproof bowl, and beat together until well blended. Put the light cream and chocolate in a saucepan and heat gently until the chocolate has melted, then continue to heat, stirring constantly, until almost boiling. Pour onto the egg mixture, stirring vigorously, then place the bowl over a saucepan of simmering water. Cook, stirring constantly, until the mixture lightly coats the back of the spoon. Strain into another bowl and let cool. Place the heavy cream in a bowl and whisk until slightly thickened, then fold into the cooled chocolate mixture.

Either freeze in an ice-cream maker, following the manufacturer's directions, or pour the mixture into a freezerproof container, cover, and freeze for 2 hours until just frozen. Spoon into a bowl and beat with a fork to break down the ice crystals. Return to the freezer until almost solid. Line the bombe mold with the chocolate ice cream and return to the freezer. Transfer from the freezer to the refrigerator 30 minutes before serving.

To make the white chocolate ice cream, put the chocolate and half the milk in a saucepan and heat gently until the chocolate has just melted. Remove from the heat and stir. Put the sugar and remaining milk in another saucepan and heat gently until the sugar has melted. Set aside to cool, then stir into the cooled white chocolate mixture. Place the cream in a bowl and whisk until slightly thickened, then fold into the chocolate mixture. Spoon into the center of the bombe, cover, and freeze for about 4 hours, until firm. To serve, dip the mold briefly into warm water, then turn out onto a serving plate. Decorate with chocolate shapes.

SEMISWEET CHOCOLATE ICE CREAM
2 eggs
2 egg yolks
½ cup superfine sugar
1¼ cups light cream
8 oz/225 g semisweet chocolate, chopped
1¼ cups heavy cream

WHITE CHOCOLATE ICE CREAM
5 oz/140 g white chocolate, broken into pieces
⅔ cup milk
2 oz/55 g superfine sugar
1¼ cups heavy cream
chocolate shapes, to decorate

Chocolate Ice Cream Bites

SERVES 6

Line a cookie sheet with plastic wrap.

Using a melon baller, scoop out balls of ice cream and place them on the prepared cookie sheet. Alternatively, cut the ice cream into bite-size cubes. Stick a toothpick in each piece and return to the freezer until very hard.

Place the chocolate and the butter in a heatproof bowl set over a saucepan of gently simmering water until melted. Quickly dip the frozen ice-cream balls or cubes into the warm chocolate and return to the freezer. Keep them there until ready to serve.

2½ cups good-quality ice cream
7 oz/200 g semisweet chocolate
2 tbsp unsalted butter

Rich Chocolate Mousses

MAKES 4

Break the chocolate into small pieces and put it in a heatproof bowl over a saucepan of gently simmering water. Add the superfine sugar and butter and melt together, stirring, until smooth. Remove from the heat, stir in the cognac, and let cool a little. Add the egg yolks and beat until smooth.

In a separate bowl, whisk the egg whites until stiff peaks form, then fold them into the chocolate mixture. Place a stainless steel cooking ring on each of 4 small serving plates, then spoon the mixture into each ring and smooth the surfaces. Transfer to the refrigerator and chill for at least 4 hours, until set.

Remove the mousses from the refrigerator and discard the cooking rings. Dust with unsweetened cocoa and serve immediately.

10^1/$_2$ oz/300 g semisweet chocolate
  (at least 70% cocoa solids)
5 tbsp superfine sugar
1^1/$_2$ tbsp unsalted butter
1 tbsp cognac
4 eggs, separated
unsweetened cocoa, for dusting

Tiramisù Layers

MAKES 6

Whip the cream until it just holds its shape. Beat the mascarpone to soften slightly, then fold in the whipped cream. Melt the chocolate in a heatproof bowl set over a saucepan of simmering water, stirring occasionally. Let the chocolate cool slightly, then stir it into the mascarpone and cream.

Mix the hot coffee and sugar in a saucepan and stir until dissolved. Let cool, then add the dark rum. Dip the ladyfingers into the mixture briefly so that they absorb the coffee and rum mixture, but do not become soggy.

Place 3 ladyfingers on each of 6 serving plates.

Spoon a layer of the chocolate, mascarpone, and cream mixture over the ladyfingers.

Place 3 more ladyfingers crosswise on top of the chocolate and mascarpone mixture. Spread another layer of chocolate and mascarpone and place 3 more ladyfingers on top.

Let the Tiramisù chill in the refrigerator for at least 1 hour. Dust with a little unsweetened cocoa just before serving.

⅔ cup heavy cream
1¾ cups mascarpone cheese
10 oz/280 g semisweet chocolate
1¾ cups hot black coffee
¼ cup superfine sugar
6 tbsp dark rum or cognac
54 ladyfingers
unsweetened cocoa, for dusting

White Chocolate Terrine

SERVES 8

Line a 1-lb/450-g loaf pan with foil or plastic wrap, pressing out as many creases as you can.

Place the granulated sugar and water in a heavy-bottom saucepan and heat gently, stirring, until the sugar has dissolved. Bring to a boil and boil for 1–2 minutes until syrupy, then remove from the heat.

Break the white chocolate into small pieces and stir it into the hot syrup, continuing to stir until the chocolate has melted and combined with the syrup. Let the mixture cool slightly.

Beat the egg yolks into the chocolate mixture. Let cool completely.

Lightly whip the cream until it is just holding its shape, and fold it into the chocolate mixture.

Whip the egg whites in a greasefree bowl until soft peaks form. Fold the whites into the chocolate mixture. Pour into the prepared loaf pan and freeze overnight.

To serve, remove the terrine from the freezer about 10–15 minutes before serving. Turn out of the pan and cut into slices. Serve with fruit coulis and strawberries.

2 tbsp granulated sugar
5 tbsp water
10 oz/280 g white chocolate
3 eggs, separated
1^1/4 cups heavy cream

TO SERVE
fruit coulis
fresh strawberries

Chocolate & Orange Slices

SERVES 8

Lightly grease a 1-lb/450-g terrine or loaf pan and line it with plastic wrap. Put the chocolate in a heatproof bowl set over a saucepan of gently simmering water. Stir over a low heat until melted. Remove from the heat and let cool slightly.

Meanwhile, peel the fruit, removing all traces of pith. Cut the zest into very thin strips. Beat the egg yolks into the chocolate, one at a time, then add most of the zest (reserve the rest for decoration) and all the sour cream and raisins, and beat until thoroughly combined. Spoon the mixture into the prepared pan, cover with plastic wrap, and chill in the refrigerator for 3–4 hours, until set.

To serve, remove the saucepan from the refrigerator and turn out the chocolate mold. Remove the plastic wrap and cut the mold into slices. Place a slice on individual serving plates and add whipped cream to serve. Decorate with the remaining zest.

2 tsp unsalted butter,
for greasing
14 oz/400 g semisweet
chocolate, broken into pieces
3 small, loose-skinned citrus
fruit such as oranges,
tangerines, or mandarins
4 egg yolks
scant 1 cup sour cream
2 tbsp raisins
1¼ cups whipped cream,
to serve

Chocolate Hazelnut Parfait

MAKES 6

Preheat the broiler to medium. Spread out the hazelnuts on a cookie sheet and toast under the broiler for about 5 minutes, shaking the sheet from time to time, until golden all over. Set aside to cool.

Put the chocolate in a heatproof bowl set over a saucepan of gently simmering water. Stir over low heat until melted, then remove from the heat and cool. Put the toasted hazelnuts in a food processor and process until finely ground.

Whip the cream until it is stiff, then fold in the ground hazelnuts and set aside. Add 3 tablespoons of the sugar to the egg yolks and beat for 10 minutes until pale and thick.

Whip the egg whites in a separate bowl until soft peaks form. Whisk in the remaining sugar, a little at a time, until the whites are stiff and glossy. Stir the cooled chocolate into the egg yolk mixture, then fold in the cream and finally, fold in the egg whites. Divide the mixture among 6 freezerproof timbales or molds, cover with plastic wrap, and freeze for at least 8 hours, or overnight, until firm.

Transfer the parfaits to the refrigerator about 10 minutes before serving to soften slightly. Turn out onto individual serving plates, dust the tops lightly with unsweetened cocoa, decorate with mint sprigs, and serve with wafers.

1½ cups blanched hazelnuts

6 oz/175 g semisweet chocolate, broken into small pieces

2½ cups heavy cream

2½ cups confectioners' sugar

3 eggs, separated

1 tbsp unsweetened cocoa, for dusting

6 small fresh mint sprigs, to decorate

wafer cookies, to serve

Cherry & Chocolate Meringue

SERVES 4

Preheat the oven to 275°F/140°C. Line a cookie sheet with parchment paper.

Whip the egg whites until stiff. Gradually add the sugar, and whip until stiff and shiny. Fold in the cornstarch, vinegar, cocoa, and chocolate. Spread the meringue onto the cookie sheet to form a 9^1/2-inch/24-cm disk. Make a hollow in the center. Bake for 1^1/2 hours.

Turn off the oven and leave the meringue in the oven for 45 minutes.

For the topping, whip the cream and confectioners' sugar until stiff, then chill in the refrigerator. Pit most of the cherries, reserving a few whole. Melt the maple syrup with the butter in a skillet and stir in the pitted cherries to coat, then set aside.

Peel off the paper from the meringue when cooled.

To serve, put the meringue on a dish. Spoon the cream into the center, pile on the cherries, using the whole ones around the edges. Top with the caraque.

4 large egg whites
1 cup superfine sugar
1 tsp cornstarch, sifted
1 tsp white wine vinegar
1 tbsp unsweetened cocoa
5 oz/140 g semisweet chocolate, chopped

TOPPING
1^3/4 cups heavy cream
^{1}/4 cup confectioners' sugar, sifted
1 lb/450 g black cherries
4 tbsp maple syrup
4 tbsp unsalted butter
semisweet chocolate caraque, to decorate

Deep Chocolate Cheesecake

SERVES 4–6

Grease an 8-inch/20-cm springform cake pan.

To make the bottom layer, put the crushed graham crackers, sugar, cocoa, and melted butter into a large bowl and mix well. Press the mixture evenly over the bottom of the prepared pan.

For the chocolate layer, put the mascarpone and sugar into a bowl and stir in the orange juice and zest. Add the melted chocolate and the brandy, and mix together until thoroughly combined. Spread the chocolate mixture evenly over the crumb layer. Cover with plastic wrap and chill for at least 4 hours.

Remove the cheesecake from the refrigerator, turn out onto a serving platter, and serve immediately.

BOTTOM LAYER

4 tbsp unsalted butter, melted, plus extra for greasing

1 cup (about 14 squares) finely crushed graham crackers

2 tbsp sugar

2 tsp unsweetened cocoa

CHOCOLATE LAYER

1 lb 12 oz/800 g mascarpone cheese

1 1/2 cups confectioners' sugar, sifted

juice of 1/2 orange

finely grated zest of 1 orange

6 oz/175 g dark chocolate, melted

2 tbsp brandy

Brownie Bottom Cheesecake

SERVES 12

Preheat the oven to 350°F/180°C. Lightly grease and flour a 9-inch/23-cm springform cake pan.

Melt the butter and the chocolate in a pan over low heat, stirring frequently, until smooth. Remove from the heat and beat in the sugar.

Add the eggs and milk, beating well. Stir in the flour, mixing just until blended. Spoon into the prepared pan, spreading evenly.

Bake for 25 minutes. Remove from the oven while preparing the topping. Reduce the oven temperature to 325°F/160°C.

For the topping, beat together the cream cheese, sugar, eggs, and vanilla extract until well blended. Stir in the yogurt, then pour over the brownie base. Bake for another 45–55 minutes, or until the center is almost set.

Run a knife around the edge of the cake to loosen from the pan. Let cool before removing from the pan. Chill in the refrigerator for 4 hours or overnight before cutting into slices. Serve drizzled with melted chocolate.

BROWNIE BOTTOM LAYER
½ cup unsalted butter, plus
 extra for greasing
4 oz/115 g bittersweet chocolate,
 broken into pieces
1 cup superfine sugar
2 eggs, beaten
¼ cup milk
1 cup all-purpose flour, plus
 extra for dusting

TOPPING
2¼ cups cream cheese
 or farmer's cheese
⅔ cup superfine sugar
3 eggs, beaten
1 tsp vanilla extract
½ cup plain yogurt
semisweet chocolate, melted,
 to drizzle

Chocolate Trifle

SERVES 8

Cut the cake into slices and make "sandwiches" with the raspberry jelly. Cut the "sandwiches" into cubes and place in a large glass serving bowl. Sprinkle with amaretto. Spread the fruit over the cake.

To make the custard, put the egg yolks and sugar in a bowl and whisk until thick and pale. Stir in the cornstarch. Put the milk in a saucepan and heat until almost boiling. Pour onto the yolk mixture, stirring. Return the mixture to the saucepan and bring just to a boil, stirring constantly, until it thickens. Remove from the heat and let cool slightly. Put the chocolate in a heatproof bowl set over a saucepan of gently simmering water until melted, then add to the custard. Pour over the cake and fruit. Cool, cover, and chill for 2 hours to set.

For the topping, put the cream in a bowl and whip until soft peaks form. Beat in the sugar and vanilla extract. Spoon over the trifle. Decorate with truffles and chocolate shapes and chill until ready to serve.

10 oz/280 g store-bought
   chocolate loaf cake
3–4 tbsp seedless raspberry jelly
4 tbsp amaretto
9 oz/250 g package frozen
   mixed red fruits, thawed

CHOCOLATE CUSTARD
6 egg yolks
1/4 cup superfine sugar
1 tbsp cornstarch
2 cups milk
2 oz/55 g semisweet chocolate,
   broken into pieces

TOPPING
1 cup heavy cream
1 tbsp superfine sugar
1/2 tsp vanilla extract

TO DECORATE
prepared chocolate truffles
chocolate shapes

Chocolate Rum Pots

MAKES 6

Put the chocolate in a heatproof bowl set over a saucepan of gently simmering water until melted. Let cool slightly.

Whisk the egg yolks with the superfine sugar in a bowl until very pale and fluffy.

Drizzle the melted chocolate into the mixture and fold in together with the rum and the heavy cream.

Whisk the egg whites in a greasefree bowl until soft peaks form. Fold the egg whites into the chocolate mixture in 2 batches. Divide the mixture among 6 individual dishes, and let chill for at least 2 hours.

To serve, decorate with a little whipped cream and marbled chocolate shapes.

8 oz/225 g semisweet chocolate
4 eggs, separated
⅓ cup superfine sugar
4 tbsp dark rum
4 tbsp heavy cream

TO DECORATE
whipped cream
marbled chocolate shapes

Chocolate Mint Swirls

MAKES 2

Place the cream in a large mixing bowl and whip until soft peaks form.

Fold in the mascarpone cheese and confectioners' sugar, then place about one-third of the mixture in a smaller bowl. Stir the crème de menthe into the smaller bowl. Put the semisweet chocolate in a heatproof bowl set over a saucepan of barely simmering water until melted. Stir the melted chocolate into the remaining mascarpone mixture.

Place alternate tablespoonfuls of the 2 mixtures into serving glasses, then swirl the mixture together to give a decorative effect. Chill until ready to serve.

To make the piped chocolate decorations, melt a small amount of chocolate and place in a paper pastry bag.

Place a sheet of parchment paper on a cutting board and pipe squiggles, stars, or flower shapes with the melted chocolate. Alternatively, to make curved decorations, pipe decorations onto a long strip of parchment paper, then carefully place the strip over a rolling pin, securing with sticky tape. Let the chocolate set, then carefully remove from the parchment paper.

Decorate each dessert with the piped chocolate decorations and serve. The desserts can be decorated and then chilled, if you prefer.

1¼ cups heavy cream
⅔ cup mascarpone cheese
2 tbsp confectioners' sugar
1 tbsp crème de menthe
6 oz/175 g semisweet chocolate,
   plus extra to decorate

Chocolate & Vanilla Creams

MAKES 4

Place the cream and sugar in a saucepan, then add the vanilla bean. Heat gently, stirring until the sugar has dissolved, then bring to a boil. Reduce the heat and simmer for 2–3 minutes.

Remove the saucepan from the heat and take out the vanilla bean. Stir in the sour cream.

Sprinkle the gelatin over the water in a small heatproof bowl and let it get absorbed, then set over a saucepan of hot water and stir until dissolved. Stir into the cream mixture. Pour half of this mixture into another mixing bowl.

Put the semisweet chocolate in a heatproof bowl over a saucepan of gently simmering water until melted. Stir the melted chocolate into half of the cream mixture. Pour the chocolate mixture into 4 individual glass serving dishes and let chill for 15–20 minutes, until just set. While it is chilling, keep the vanilla mixture at room temperature.

Spoon the vanilla mixture on top of the chocolate mixture and let chill until the vanilla is set. Decorate with chocolate shavings.

scant 2 cups heavy cream
$\frac{1}{3}$ cup superfine sugar
1 vanilla bean
$\frac{3}{4}$ cup sour cream
2 tsp powdered gelatin
3 tbsp water
1$\frac{3}{4}$ oz/50 g semisweet chocolate
chocolate caraque, to decorate

Raspberry Chocolate Boxes

MAKES 12

To make the mocha mousse, melt 2 oz/55 g of the chocolate in a heatproof bowl set over a saucepan of gently simmering water. Add the coffee and stir over low heat until smooth, then remove from the heat and cool slightly. Stir in the egg yolk and the Kahlúa. Whisk the egg whites in a separate bowl until stiff peaks form. Fold into the chocolate mixture, cover with plastic wrap, and chill for 2 hours, until set.

For the sponge cake, lightly grease an 8-inch/20-cm square cake pan and line with parchment paper. Put the egg and extra white with the sugar in a heatproof bowl set over a saucepan of gently simmering water. Whisk over low heat for 5–10 minutes, until pale and thick. Remove from the heat and continue whisking for 10 minutes until cooled and a trail is left when the whisk is dragged across the surface.

Preheat the oven to 350°F/180°C. Sift the flour over the egg mixture and gently fold it in. Pour the mixture into the prepared pan and spread evenly. Bake in the preheated oven for 20–25 minutes, until firm to the touch and slightly shrunk from the sides of the saucepan. Turn out onto a wire rack to cool, then invert the cake, keeping the parchment paper in place.

To make the chocolate boxes, grease a 12 x 9–inch/30 x 23–cm jelly roll pan and line with wax paper. Place the remaining chocolate in a heatproof bowl set over a saucepan of gently simmering water. Stir over low heat until melted, but not too runny. Pour it into the jelly roll pan and spread evenly with a spatula. Set aside in a cool place for about 30 minutes, until set.

Turn out the set chocolate onto parchment paper on a counter. Cut it into 36 rectangles, measuring 3 x 1 inches/7.5 x 2.5 cm. Cut 12 of these rectangles in half to make 24 rectangles measuring 1½ x 1 inches/4 x 2.5 cm.

Trim the crusty edges off the sponge cake, then cut it into 12 slices, measuring 3 x 1¼ inches/7.5 x 3 cm. Spread a little of the mocha mousse along the sides of each sponge rectangle and press 2 long and 2 short chocolate rectangles in place on each side to make boxes. Divide the remaining mousse among the boxes and top with raspberries. Chill until ready to use.

MOCHA MOUSSE

7 oz/200 g semisweet chocolate,
  broken into pieces
1½ tsp cold, strong, black coffee
1 egg yolk
1½ tsp Kahlúa or other
  coffee-flavored liqueur
2 egg whites
¾ cup raspberries, to decorate

SPONGE CAKE

2 tsp unsalted butter, for
  greasing
1 egg, plus 1 egg white
¼ cup superfine sugar
scant ½ cup all-purpose flour

Cool Minty Chocolate

SERVES 6

Pour half the milk into a small saucepan and stir in the drinking chocolate powder. Heat gently, stirring constantly, until just below boiling point and the mixture is smooth. Remove the saucepan from the heat.

Pour the chocolate-flavored milk into a large, chilled bowl and whisk in the remaining milk. Whisk in the cream and peppermint extract and continue to whisk until cold.

Pour the mixture into 6 glasses, top each with a scoop of ice cream, decorate with a mint sprig, and serve immediately.

2¹/₂ cups ice-cold milk
6 tbsp drinking chocolate
  powder
1 cup light cream
1 tsp peppermint extract
6 scoops chocolate-mint
  ice cream
fresh mint sprigs, to decorate

Chocolate Milk Shakes

SERVES 4

Pour the milk, chocolate syrup, and coffee syrup into a food processor and gently process until blended. Add the ice cream and process to a smooth consistency.

Pour into 4 glasses.

To decorate, spoon the cream into a pastry bag with a large, star-shaped tip. Pipe generous amounts of cream on top of the milk shakes. Sprinkle over the cocoa and serve with straws.

1¼ cups milk
2 tbsp chocolate syrup
2 tbsp coffee syrup
1¼–1½ pints chocolate ice cream

TO DECORATE
⅔ cup heavy cream, whipped
unsweetened cocoa, for dusting

Little Treats & Luxury Drinks

Chocolate Almond Petits Fours

MAKES 15

Preheat the oven to 375°F/190°C. Line a cookie sheet with parchment paper. Put the ground almonds, sugar, and unsweetened cocoa in a bowl and mix together well. Add the egg white and mix to form a firm mixture.

Fill a pastry bag, fitted with a small plain tip, with the mixture and pipe 2-inch/5-cm lengths, spaced well apart, onto the prepared cookie sheet. Place an almond half on top of each.

Bake in the oven for about 5 minutes, until firm. Transfer to a wire rack and let cool.

When the petits fours have cooled, melt the chocolate in a heatproof bowl set over a saucepan of gently simmering water. Dip each end of the petits fours into the melted chocolate, then let stand on the wire rack to set.

½ cup ground almonds
½ cup granulated sugar
5 tsp unsweetened cocoa
1 egg white
8 blanched almonds, halved
2 oz/55 g semisweet chocolate, broken into pieces

Ginger Chocolate Fudge

MAKES AROUND 50 PIECES

Grease a 7-inch/18-cm shallow square pan or an 8 x 6-inch/20 x 15-cm shallow pan. Dry the syrup off the pieces of preserved ginger on paper towels, then chop finely.

Pour the milk into a large, heavy-bottom saucepan and add the chocolate, butter, and sugar. Heat gently, stirring all the time, until the chocolate and butter have melted and the sugar has dissolved.

Bring to a boil and then boil for about 10–15 minutes, stirring occasionally, until a little of the mixture, when dropped into a small bowl of cold water, forms a soft ball when rolled between your fingers.

Remove the saucepan from the heat and stir in the chopped ginger. Let cool for 5 minutes, then beat the mixture vigorously with a wooden spoon until thick, creamy, and grainy.

Immediately pour the mixture into the prepared saucepan, let cool, then mark into small squares. Leave the fudge until cooled and set, then cut up the squares with a sharp knife. Decorate with pieces of preserved ginger.

^{1}/2 cup unsalted butter, plus
   extra for greasing
6 pieces preserved ginger,
   plus extra to decorate
1^{1}/4 cups milk
5^{1}/2 oz/150 g bittersweet
   chocolate, broken into pieces
2^{1}/3 cups granulated sugar

Fruit & Nut Fudge

MAKES 36 PIECES

Lightly grease an 8-inch/20-cm square cake pan.

Put the chocolate in a heatproof bowl with the butter and evaporated milk and set over a saucepan of gently simmering water. Stir until the chocolate and butter melt and the mixture is well blended.

Remove the bowl from the heat and gradually beat in the confectioners' sugar. Stir the hazelnuts and golden raisins into the mixture. Press the fudge into the prepared pan and smooth the top. Chill until firm.

Turn the fudge out onto a cutting board and cut into squares. Chill in the refrigerator until ready to serve.

2 tbsp unsalted butter, plus
 extra for greasing
9 oz/250 g semisweet chocolate,
 broken into pieces
4 tbsp evaporated milk
3 cups confectioners' sugar,
 sifted
½ cup coarsely chopped
 hazelnuts
⅓ cup golden raisins

Chocolate Creams

MAKES ABOUT 30

Line a cookie sheet with parchment paper. Melt 2 oz/55 g of the chocolate in a large heatproof bowl set over a saucepan of gently simmering water. Stir in the cream and remove the bowl from the heat.

Sift the confectioners' sugar into the melted chocolate then, using a fork, mix well together. Knead to form a firm, smooth, pliable mixture.

Lightly dust a counter with drinking chocolate powder, turn out the mixture, and roll out to $^1/4$-inch/5-mm thickness, then cut into circles, using a 1-inch/2.5-cm plain round cutter.

Transfer to the prepared cookie sheet and let stand for about 12 hours, or overnight, until set and dry.

When the chocolate creams have set, line a cookie sheet with parchment paper. Melt the remaining chocolate in a heatproof bowl set over a saucepan of gently simmering water. Using 2 forks, carefully dip each chocolate cream into the melted chocolate. Lift them out quickly, letting any excess chocolate drain against the side of the bowl, and place on the prepared cookie sheet. Let set.

7 oz/200 g semisweet chocolate,
   broken into pieces
2 tbsp light cream
2 cups confectioners' sugar

Nutty Chocolate Clusters

MAKES 30

Line a cookie sheet with parchment paper. Put the white chocolate in a large heatproof bowl set over a saucepan of gently simmering water and stir until melted.

Break the graham crackers into small pieces. Stir the crackers into the melted chocolate with the chopped nuts and the preserved ginger (if using).

Place heaping teaspoons of the mixture on the prepared cookie sheet.

Chill the mixture until set, then remove from the parchment paper.

Melt the semisweet chocolate and let it cool slightly. Dip the clusters into the melted chocolate, letting the excess drip back into the bowl. Return the clusters to the cookie sheet and chill in the refrigerator until set.

6 oz/175 g white chocolate,
  broken into pieces
3½ oz/100 g graham crackers
⅔ cup chopped macadamia
  nuts or Brazil nuts
1 oz/25 g preserved ginger,
  chopped (optional)
6 oz/175 g semisweet chocolate,
  broken into pieces

Mini Florentines

MAKES 40

Preheat the oven to 350°F/180°C. Grease and flour 2 cookie sheets or line with parchment paper.

Place the butter in a small saucepan and heat gently until melted. Add the sugar, stir until dissolved, then bring the mixture to a boil. Remove from the heat and stir in the golden raisins, cherries, ginger, sunflower seeds, and almonds. Mix well, then beat in the cream.

Place small teaspoons of the fruit and nut mixture onto the prepared cookie sheets, allowing plenty of room for the mixture to spread during baking. Bake in the preheated oven for 10–12 minutes, or until light golden in color.

Remove from the oven and, while still hot, use a circular cookie cutter to pull in the edges to form perfect circles. Leave to cool and get crisp before removing from the cookie sheets.

Put the chocolate in a heatproof bowl set over a saucepan of gently simmering water and stir until melted. Spread most of the chocolate onto a sheet of parchment paper. When the chocolate is at the point of setting, place the cookies flat-side down on the chocolate and let it harden completely.

Cut around the florentines and remove from the parchment paper. Spread a little more chocolate on the coated side of the florentines and use a fork to mark waves in the chocolate. Leave to set. Keep cool.

6 tbsp unsalted butter, plus
  extra for greasing
all-purpose flour, for dusting
6 tbsp superfine sugar
2 tbsp golden raisins
2 tbsp chopped candied cherries
2 tbsp chopped preserved ginger
1 oz/25 g sunflower seeds
3½ oz/100 g flaked almonds
2 tbsp heavy cream
6 oz/175 g semisweet or milk
  chocolate, broken into pieces

Hot Chocolate Cherries

SERVES 4

Put the water, sugar, and lemon zest into a heavy-bottom saucepan and bring to a boil over low heat, stirring constantly, until the sugar has dissolved. Add the cherries and cook, stirring constantly, for 1 minute. Remove the saucepan from the heat and, using a slotted spoon, transfer the cherries to a flameproof dish. Reserve the syrup.

Preheat the broiler to medium. Put the unsweetened cocoa in a bowl and mix in a pinch of salt. Whisking constantly, pour in the cream in a steady stream. Remove and discard the lemon zest from the syrup, then stir in the cream mixture. Return the saucepan to the heat and bring to a boil, stirring constantly. Simmer over very low heat, stirring occasionally, for 10–15 minutes, or until reduced by about half.

Remove from the heat, stir in the maraschino liqueur, and pour the sauce over the cherries. Place under the preheated broiler for 2 minutes, then serve.

4 tbsp water
¹/₄ cup superfine sugar
1 strip pared lemon zest
1 lb/450 g sweet black cherries, pitted
1 tbsp unsweetened cocoa
salt
4 tbsp heavy cream
4 tbsp maraschino liqueur or cherry cognac

White Chocolate Truffles

MAKES 20

Line a jelly roll pan with parchment paper.

Place the butter and cream in a small saucepan and bring slowly to a boil, stirring constantly. Boil for 1 minute, then remove from the heat.

Add the Swiss white chocolate to the cream. Stir until melted, then beat in the liqueur (if using).

Pour into the prepared pan and chill for about 2 hours, until firm.

Break off pieces of the mixture and roll them into balls. Chill for an additional 30 minutes before finishing the truffles.

To finish, put the white chocolate in a heatproof bowl set over a saucepan of gently simmering water until melted. Dip the balls in the chocolate, letting the excess drip back into the bowl. Place on nonstick parchment paper, swirl the chocolate with the tines of a fork, and let it harden.

2 tbsp unsalted butter
5 tbsp heavy cream
8 oz/225 g good-quality
  Swiss white chocolate, broken
  into small pieces
1 tbsp orange-flavored
  liqueur (optional)
3½ oz/100 g white chocolate,
  broken into pieces, for coating

Italian Chocolate Truffles

MAKES 24

Melt the semisweet chocolate with the liqueur in a bowl set over a saucepan of hot water, stirring until well combined.

Add the butter and stir until it has melted. Stir in the confectioners' sugar and the ground almonds.

Let the mixture stand in a cool place until it is firm enough to roll into 24 balls.

Place the grated chocolate on a plate and roll the truffles in the chocolate to coat them.

Place the truffles in paper candy cases and let chill.

6 oz/175 g semisweet chocolate

2 tbsp amaretto liqueur or
orange flavored liqueur

3 tbsp unsalted butter

4 tbsp confectioners' sugar

1/2 cup ground almonds

1-3/4 oz/50 g semisweet
chocolate, grated, to decorate

Chocolate Liqueurs

MAKES 20

Line a cookie sheet with parchment paper. Break the semisweet chocolate into pieces, place in a bowl and set over a saucepan of hot water. Stir until melted. Spoon the chocolate into 20 paper candy cases, spreading up the sides with a small spoon or brush. Place upside down on the cookie sheet and let set.

Carefully peel away the paper cases. Place a cherry half or nut in the bottom of each cup.

To make the filling, place the heavy cream in a mixing bowl and sift the confectioners' sugar on top. Whip the cream until it is just holding its shape, then whisk in the liqueur to flavor it.

Place the cream in a pastry bag fitted with a ½-inch/1-cm plain tip and pipe a little into each chocolate case. Let chill for 20 minutes.

To finish, spoon the semisweet chocolate over the cream to cover it. Add the caraque and let harden.

3½ oz/100 g semisweet chocolate
about 5 candied cherries, halved
about 10 hazelnuts or macadamia nuts
⅔ cup heavy cream
2 tbsp confectioners' sugar
4 tbsp liqueur

TO FINISH
1¾ oz/50 g semisweet chocolate, melted
marbled chocolate caraque, to decorate

Rum & Chocolate Cups

MAKES 12

To make the chocolate cups, place the semisweet chocolate in the top of a double boiler or in a heatproof bowl set over a saucepan of barely simmering water. Stir over low heat until the chocolate is just melted but not too runny, then remove from the heat. Spoon $1/2$ teaspoon of melted chocolate into a foil confectionery case and brush it over the bottom and up the sides. Coat 11 more foil cases in the same way and let set for 30 minutes, then let chill in the refrigerator for 15 minutes. If necessary, reheat the chocolate in the double boiler or heatproof bowl to melt it again, then coat the foil cases with a second, slightly thinner coating. Chill in the refrigerator for an additional 30 minutes.

To make the filling, place the chocolate in the top of a double boiler or in a heatproof bowl set over a saucepan of barely simmering water. Stir over low heat until melted and smooth, then remove from the heat. Let cool slightly, stir in the rum, and beat in the mascarpone cheese until smooth. Let cool completely, stirring occasionally.

Spoon the filling into a pastry bag fitted with a $1/2$-inch/1-cm star tip. Carefully peel away the confectionery cases from the chocolate cups. Pipe the filling into the cups and top each one with a toasted hazelnut.

2 oz/55 g semisweet chocolate, broken into pieces
12 hazelnuts, toasted

FILLING

4 oz/115 g semisweet chocolate, broken into pieces
1 tbsp dark rum
4 tbsp mascarpone cheese

Rocky Road Bites

MAKES 18

Line a cookie sheet with parchment paper and set aside.

Break the chocolate into small pieces and place in a large heatproof bowl. Set the bowl over a saucepan of simmering water and stir until the chocolate has melted.

Stir in the marshmallows, walnuts, and apricots, and toss in the melted chocolate until well covered.

Place heaping teaspoons of the marshmallow mixture onto the prepared cookie sheet, then let chill in the refrigerator until set.

Once they are set, carefully remove from the parchment paper.

Place in paper candy cases to serve, if desired.

4¹/₂ oz/125 g milk chocolate
1³/₄ oz/50 g mini multicolored
  marshmallows
¹/₄ cup chopped walnuts
1 oz/25 g plumped dried
  apricots, chopped

Apricot & Almond Clusters

MAKES 24–28

Place the chocolate and honey in a heatproof bowl and set over a saucepan of gently simmering water until the chocolate has melted.

Stir the apricots and almonds into the melted chocolate mixture.

Drop teaspoonfuls of the mixture into petit-four cases. Let set for 2–4 hours, or until firm. Serve.

4 oz/115 g semisweet chocolate, broken into pieces

2 tbsp honey

⅔ cup plumped dried apricots, chopped

scant ½ cup chopped blanched almonds

Brazil Nut Brittle

MAKES 20

Brush the bottom of an 8-inch/20-cm square cake pan with oil and line with parchment paper. Melt half the semisweet chocolate in a heatproof bowl over a saucepan of gently simmering water and spread in the prepared pan.

Sprinkle with the chopped Brazil nuts, white chocolate, and fudge. Melt the remaining semisweet chocolate pieces and pour over the top.

Let the brittle set, then break up into jagged pieces using the tip of a strong knife.

sunflower oil, for brushing

12 oz/350 g semisweet chocolate, broken into pieces

scant ¾ cup chopped Brazil nuts

6 oz/175 g white chocolate, coarsely chopped

6 oz/175 g fudge, coarsely chopped

Chocolate Fondue

SERVES 6

Using a sharp knife, peel and core the pineapple, then cut the flesh into cubes. Peel the mango and cut the flesh into cubes. Peel back the papery outer skin of the cape gooseberries and twist at the top to make a handle. Arrange all the fruit on 6 serving plates and leave to chill in the refrigerator.

To make the fondue, place the chocolate and cream in a fondue pot. Heat gently, stirring constantly, until the chocolate has melted. Stir in the brandy until thoroughly blended and the chocolate mixture is smooth.

Place the fondue pot over the burner to keep warm. To serve, let each guest dip the fruit into the sauce, using fondue forks or bamboo skewers.

1 pineapple
1 mango
12 cape gooseberries
    (if unavailable, use 12 small
    cubes of firm sponge cake
    instead)
9 oz/250 g fresh strawberries
9 oz/250 g seedless green
    grapes

FONDUE
9 oz/250 g semisweet chocolate,
    broken into pieces
150 ml/5 fl oz heavy cream
2 tbsp brandy

French Chocolate Sauce

MAKES ²/₃ CUP

Bring the cream gently to a boil in a small, heavy-bottom saucepan over low heat. Remove the saucepan from the heat, add the chocolate and stir until smooth.

Stir in the liqueur and serve immediately, or keep the sauce warm until ready to serve. Serve over ice cream.

6 tbsp heavy cream
3 oz/85 g semisweet chocolate, broken into small pieces
2 tbsp orange-flavored liqueur
ice cream, to serve

Chocolate Fudge Sauce

MAKES SCANT 1 CUP

Pour the cream into the top of a double boiler or a heatproof bowl set over a saucepan of barely simmering water. Add the butter and sugar and stir until the mixture is smooth. Remove from the heat.

Stir in the chocolate, a few pieces at a time, waiting until each batch has melted before adding the next. Add the cognac and stir the sauce until smooth. Cool to room temperature before serving.

²⁄₃ cup heavy cream

4 tbsp unsalted butter, cut into small pieces

3 tbsp superfine sugar

6 oz/175 g white chocolate, broken into pieces

2 tbsp cognac

Real Hot Chocolate

SERVES 1–2

Place the chocolate in a large, heatproof pitcher. Place the milk in a heavy-bottom saucepan and bring to a boil. Pour about one-quarter of the milk onto the chocolate and leave until the chocolate has softened.

Whisk the milk and chocolate mixture until smooth. Return the remaining milk to the heat and return to a boil, then pour onto the chocolate, whisking constantly.

Pour into warmed mugs or cups and top with the chocolate curls. Serve immediately.

1¹/₂ oz/40 g semisweet chocolate, broken into pieces
1¹/₄ cups milk
chocolate curls, to decorate

Hot Chocolate Float

SERVES 4

Pour the milk into a saucepan. Break the chocolate into pieces and add to the saucepan with the sugar. Stir over low heat until the chocolate has melted, the sugar has dissolved, and the mixture is smooth. Remove the saucepan from the heat.

Put 1 scoop of coconut ice cream into each of 4 heatproof glasses, top with a scoop of chocolate ice cream, then repeat the layers.

Pour the chocolate-flavored milk into the glasses, top with whipped cream, and serve immediately.

2 cups milk

8 oz/225 g semisweet chocolate

2 tbsp superfine sugar

8 scoops coconut ice cream

8 scoops semisweet chocolate ice cream

whipped cream, to decorate

Cinnamon Mocha

SERVES 6

Put the chocolate in a large heatproof bowl set over a saucepan of gently simmering water. Add the light cream and stir until the chocolate has melted and the mixture is smooth.

Pour in the coffee, add the cinnamon, and whisk until foamy. If serving hot, pour into heatproof glasses or mugs, top with cream and marbled chocolate caraque, and serve immediately. If serving cold, remove the bowl from the heat and let cool, chill in the refrigerator until ready to serve, then decorate with whipped cream and caraque.

9 oz/250 g milk chocolate,
   broken into pieces
¾ cup light cream
4½ cups freshly brewed coffee
1 tsp ground cinnamon

TO DECORATE
whipped cream
marbled chocolate caraque

Marshmallow Float

SERVES 4

Finely chop the chocolate with a knife or in a food processor. Do not over-process or the chocolate will melt.

Pour the milk into a saucepan and bring to just below the boiling point. Remove the saucepan from the heat and whisk in the sugar and the chocolate.

Pour into warmed mugs or heatproof glasses, top with a marshmallow or two and serve immediately.

8 oz/225 g semisweet chocolate,
    broken into pieces
3 ¾ cups milk
3 tbsp superfine sugar
8 marshmallows

INDEX